AQA English and English Language

Higher Tier

Revision Guide

GCSE

Author and Series Editor
Imelda Pilgrim

D0413573

ornes

Text © Imelda Pilgrim 2010
Original illustrations © Nelson Thornes 2010

The right of Imelda Pilgrim to be identified as author of this work has been asserted by her in accordance with the Copyright, Designs and Patents Act 1988.

All rights reserved. No part of this publication may be reproduced or transmitted in any form or by any means, electronic or mechanical, including photocopy, recording or any information storage and retrieval system, without permission in writing from the publisher or under licence from the Copyright Licensing Agency Limited, of Saffron House, 6–10 Kirby Street, London, EC1N 8TS.

Any person who commits any unauthorised act in relation to this publication may be liable to criminal prosecution and civil claims for damages.

Published in 2010 by:
Nelson Thornes Ltd
Delta Place
27 Bath Road
CHELTENHAM
GL53 7TH
United Kingdom

11 12 13 14 / 10 9 8 7 6 5 4 3 2

A catalogue record for this book is available from the British Library

ISBN 978 1 4085 0691 2

Illustrations by Alan Rowe; Harry Venning; Seb Camagajevac (Beehive Illustration); Paul McCaffrey

Cover photograph by Heather Gunn Photography

Page make-up by Pantek Arts Ltd, Maidstone

Printed and bound in China by 1010 Printing International Ltd

DUDLEY PUBLIC
LIBRARIES

000000553578

Bertrams	01/11/2012
428	£6.99
	BH

The authors and publishers wish to thank the following for permission to use copyright material:

Text: p3 (also pp 19, 33, 35) 'Seattle: Gateway to your Washington State adventure' Seattle Conventions and Visitors Bureau; p9 (also pp 23, 39) 'Washington State: Green before green was cool' Washington State Tourism; p10 (also pp 19, 33, 37) 'True Tribal Style' by Anna Webber, published in *Wanderlust*, April/May 2009. Photos by Hans Silvester/Rapho, Camera Press London; p17 (also pp 23, 39) Review of Tony Hawk Ride, www.gamespot.com/ ps3/sports/tonyhawkride/review.html, courtesy of CBS Interactive Inc.; p25 '"Mass overdose" homeopathy protest at Boots' by Sam Jones, *The Guardian*, 30 January 2010. Copyright Guardian News & Media Ltd 2010; p26 (also pp 28 (in part), 33, 35, 37), 'Mindless in Gaza' by Jack Shamash, *The Weekend Guardian*, 12 October 1991. Copyright Guardian News & Media Ltd 2010; p31 (also p39)'Wild Thoughts' by Mark Carwardine, reproduced courtesy of Mark Carwardine; page 41 (also pp 44, 47) homepage of the Shakespeare Schools Festival, www.ssf.uk.com; p42 (also pp 45, 47) Shakespeare's Houses and Gardens leaflet, reproduced courtesy of the Shakespeare Birthplace Trust; p49 'Famine in Ethiopia' by Michael Buerk; Unicef leaflet 'We promise, will you?' Unicef; p50 'Gates gives billions for vaccines to save millions' by Sarah Boseley, *The Guardian*, 30 January 2010. Copyright Guardian News & Media Ltd 2010; p74 extract from *The Kite Runner* by Khaled Hosseini, Bloomsbury, 2004.

Photos: p1 Martin Mayer/Alamy; p2 Remi Benali/Getty Images; p25 Cordelia Molloy/Science Photo Library; p50 Bloomberg/Getty Images; p51 Tom Merton/ Getty Images; p57 Education Photos/John Walmsley; p58 iStockphoto; p59 iStockphoto; p61 Fotolia; p63 Wildscape/Alamy; p64 Fotolia; p66 Fotolia; p67 Ryan McVay/ Getty Images; p68 iStockphoto; p70 iStockphoto; p74 Bloomsbury; p83 iStockphoto (all); p85 Jim Wileman/Alamy; p90 Profimedia International s.r.o./Alamy.

Every effort has been made to contact the copyright holders and we apologise if any have been overlooked. Should copyright have been unwittingly infringed in this book, the owners should contact the publishers, who will make corrections at reprint.

Contents

AQA GCSE English and GCSE English Language

Nelson Thornes and AQA

Nelson Thornes has worked in partnership with AQA to ensure that the revision guide and the accompanying online resources offer you the best support possible for your GCSE exam. The print and online resources together **unlock blended learning**: this means that the links between the activities in the book and the activities online blend together to maximise your understanding of a topic and help you achieve your potential.

All AQA-endorsed products undergo a thorough quality assurance process to ensure that their contents closely match the AQA specification. You can be confident that the content of materials branded with AQA's 'Exclusively Endorsed' logo have been written, checked and approved by AQA senior examiners, in order to achieve AQA's exclusive endorsement.

About your exam

This book has been written to guide you through your GCSE English or GCSE English Language exam. It will remind you of the skills you need to succeed in your exams.

How to use this book

There are two sections of the book, covering Reading and Writing. You will be assessed on each of these skills by an exam. After you've worked through each section, you are shown how to use these skills effectively when being assessed in the 'Making your skills count' chapters. There is then a chapter with a practice exam for you to try. There are also reminders about how to punctuate and spell correctly. Remember, you will gain marks for being able to spell and punctuate your work accurately.

The features in this book include:

Objectives

At the beginning of each chapter you will find a list of learning objectives that contain targets linked to the requirements of the specification.

Activity

Activities to develop and reinforce the skills focus for the chapter.

Check your revision

What you should know and be able to do. Work through the questions to check what you've learned in the chapter.

Some (but not all) chapters feature:

Practice question

Use the skills that you've just learned to answer the questions. This will make sure you know and understand the points being made about how to apply your skills in the exam.

Top Tip

Guidance on how to avoid common pitfalls and mistakes, and how to achieve the best marks in the exam.

Key terms

Key term: a term that you will find useful to be able to define and understand. The definitions also appear in the glossary at the end of the book.

Online resources

Revision guide website

For FREE online resources, go to www.nelsonthornes.com/aqagcse/revision guides.

kerboodle!

These online resources are available on which can be accessed via the internet at **www.kerboodle.com/live**, anytime, anywhere.

If your school or college subscribes to kerboodle! you will be provided with your own personal login details. Once logged in, access your course and locate the required activity.

Throughout the book you will see this icon whenever there is a relevant interactive activity available in kerboodle!

Please visit **kerboodle.helpserve.com** if you would like more information and help on how to use kerboodle!

Weblinks for this book

Because Nelson Thornes is not responsible for third party content online, there may be some changes to this material that are beyond our control. In order for us to ensure that the links referred to are as up-to-date and stable as possible, please let us know at **webadmin@ nelsonthornes.com** if you find a link that doesn't work and we will do our best to redirect these, or to list an alternative site.

Introduction

About the exam

Throughout your GCSE course you have been developing your skills in reading. These skills will help you to cope with the demands of the exam.

There is one exam paper in GCSE English and GCSE English Language. Its focus is: **understanding and producing non-fiction texts.**

The paper is divided into two sections:

- **Section A**: Reading (one hour) and worth 20% of your final marks
- **Section B:** Writing (one hour) and worth 20% of your final marks.

In Section A you will be asked to read three non-fiction items and answer four questions. There will be one question on each item. The fourth question will name one item and allow you to choose a second one. It will ask you to compare the treatment of a specific feature, such as use of language, in the two items.

The Assessment Objectives

To do well, you need to be clear what skills are being tested. These are defined in the Assessment Objectives that underpin the exam questions, and the mark scheme that examiners use to assess your answers. The Assessment Objectives are printed below. The annotations show you what they mean in terms of the skills you need to show your examiner.

Show skills such as inference, deduction, exploration and interpretation

Select and use material from two different texts in order to answer the question

Read and understand texts, selecting material appropriate to purpose, collating from different sources and making comparisons and cross references as appropriate.

Select detail in order to answer the question

Point out similarities and differences between texts, and make relevant connections between them

Make judgements on the effectiveness of the features used in the text

Consider how the writer/designer is trying to manipulate the intended reader

Explain and evaluate how writers use linguistic, grammatical, structural and presentational features to achieve effects and influence the reader, supporting comments with detailed textual references.

Focus in detail on the techniques of the writers and designers

Examine and analyse the words and the order in which they are placed, the way the text is organised and the use of presentational features such as images, colours and a range of fonts

Refer to the text in detail to support the points you make

Being prepared

When you take the exam you have one hour to complete the Reading section. The following chapters will help you to understand what is expected and ensure that you show the best of your reading skills in order to gain the most marks.

Objectives

In this chapter you will revise:

how to read with understanding

interpreting different ideas and perspectives

the use of structural and presentational features

the way language is used.

Analysing advertisements

In your English examination you may be asked to write about the ideas contained within a text and/or the ways those ideas are expressed and presented to you.

Reading with understanding

We read at different levels and in different ways. The ability to find relevant details is a basic and an essential reading skill.

Activity

1   Read Item 1.1, the advertisement called 'Seattle: Gateway to your Washington State adventure'. List four different things which, according to this advertisement, you can do in Seattle.

To answer Activity 1, you had to select relevant details from the third paragraph. You were not asked to re-word these, nor what they suggested about life in Seattle. You simply had to list them and show basic understanding.

In your exam, however, you need to demonstrate the ability to infer meaning from words, using skills of interpretation, exploration and deduction.

Activity

2   Think about and jot down notes in answer to each of the following questions about Item 1.1:

  a   What is suggested by the word 'adventure' in the title?

  b   What is suggested in the first paragraph about the different things you can do in Seattle?

  c   How do the activities listed in the third paragraph

    ● reflect the idea of 'adventure'?

    ● illustrate the claims of the first paragraph?

In Activity 2 you inferred meaning and explored connections between different parts of the text. Now think about this question:

What does the advert suggest a visitor can do in Seattle?

Here, you need to show that you are able to work out what is being 'suggested' or implied by the advertisement as a whole.

Practice question

■ Use your answers to Activities 1 and 2 to answer this question:

  a   What does the advert suggest a visitor can do in Seattle?

  b   Compare your answer with the answer on page 4. Make a note of any points you missed.

Item 1.1

SEATTLE: GATEWAY TO YOUR WASHINGTON STATE ADVENTURE.

Seattle: the perfect mix of experiences. Cosmopolitan and casual. Industrious and playful. High-tech and hand-crafted. Urban and natural.

With over 25 international flights arriving regularly, Seattle is the perfect gateway to begin your exploration of Washington, and the Pacific Northwest.

Experience the city's renowned restaurants, shops and cultural attractions. Jump on a ferry to nearby islands. Take a day trip to the mountains or the rainforests, or journey east to the high desert and wine regions. It's all here.

Oh, and we also make a pretty good cup of coffee.

To begin your journey, please visit www.ExperienceWA.com

Or contact our local representative:

ExperienceWA.com
Washington State Tourism

In the United Kingdom:
First Public Relations
Tel: +44 (20) 7978 5233
Fax: +44 (20) 7924 3134
web: www.firstpr.co.uk

In Belgium, Netherlands and Luxembourg:
BuroSix
Tel: +31 (0) 182 39 44 55
Fax: +31 (0) 654 28 03 32
info@burosix.nl
www.burosix.nl

> What does the advert suggest a visitor can do in Seattle?

The use of the word 'adventure' in the title suggests visitors to Seattle can have an exciting time and perhaps do things there that they have not done before. The first paragraph shows a wide range of types of activities or experiences, contrasting one with the other as in 'Industrious and playful' and 'Urban and natural'. This creates an impression that there is something there for everyone. This impression is supported in the third paragraph which gives specific examples of things a visitor can do. For example, for 'urban' you have the 'shops and cultural attractions' and for 'natural' you have the 'mountains and rainforests'. This list of possibilities reinforces the suggestion that there is something for everyone.

Referring to details in the text

The mark scheme used by examiners states that students should: 'Offer relevant and appropriate quotation to support clear understanding'. Look again at the student's answer to the practice question and note how often specific details in the text are referred to in order to support the points made.

Activity

3 Look again at your answer to the practice question: What does the advert suggest a visitor can do in Seattle? Underline or highlight any specific references that you made to the text.

4 Place an asterisk beside points you have made where you could have helpfully referred to the text but did not do so.

In the example above, the quotations are embedded in the student's answer to the question. This means that they are fixed within the sentences and not stuck on as an afterthought.

Commenting on structure and presentation

Structure refers to how the images and text are set out on the page.

Presentation refers to the range of presentational features that are used. The most common of these are colour, illustrations and font.

In the exam, you may be asked to comment on specific features (such as the use of colour) or to write more generally about how structural and presentational features are used. You need to be prepared for either type of question.

> **Top Tip**
>
> The ability to embed quotations is partly a writing skill. It is one you should aim to develop, as it will help you to express high-level reading skills.

Activity

5 The advertisement (Item 1.1) is organised into four distinct parts. Can you work out what they are?

6 Which part has most visual prominence? Can you suggest a reason for this?

7 Which part has least visual prominence? Can you suggest a reason for this?

Now look at this spidergram which details different features of presentation.

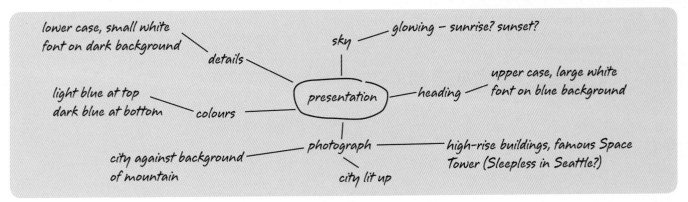

So far this student has simply identified features of presentation. In order to gain good marks in an exam he must now use his skills of inference, interpretation and deduction to say things about these features. Take, for example, the sky. The student has noted that it is glowing and could be sunset or sunrise. Here is a possible comment that the student could make. The highlighted parts show skills of inference, interpretation and deduction.

> The sky is glowing making it look like the end or the start of a nice day. The fact that we cannot tell whether it is morning or night, combined with the city lights, suggests that this is a city that never sleeps, a place where something is always happening. It also makes it feel as though it would be a good place to visit either in daytime or at night.

Practice question

2 a Using ideas from the spidergram and other ideas of your own, write a paragraph about the photograph.

b Highlight the parts of your paragraph that show skills of inference, interpretation and deduction.

Thinking about language

You need to be able to analyse use of language in the same ways as you analyse features of presentation. In the following extract a student writes about the use of adjectives in the advertisement. The highlighted parts show skills of inference, interpretation and deduction.

> In the first paragraph a series of descriptive phrases are written as sentences, presumably to give each one more impact. In these phrases adjectives are used to describe opposite aspects of Seattle. For example, in the first one 'cosmopolitan' and 'casual' are placed next to each other. The first one of these suggests fast-paced city life and the second one suggests a more relaxed and easy pace. This contrast is found again in the juxtaposition of 'urban and natural', again emphasising the contrasting sides of life in Seattle and the 'perfect mix' referred to in the opening sentence. Overall the implication is that there is something there to please everyone.

3 **a** Copy the following table. The first column names the features, the second column gives examples of them, and the third column is for comments on them. Use the example on page 6 as a model to help you complete the third column.

Feature of language use	Example(s) of feature	Comment on feature
Addresses reader directly	'your Washington State adventure', 'your exploration', 'your journey'	
Directives (also known as imperatives and command verbs)	'experience', 'jump', 'take', 'journey'	
Present tense	'Seattle is', 'we also make'	

b Highlight the parts of your comment that show skills of inference, interpretation and deduction.

There are other features of language use in the advertisement that you could have selected, such as short sentences for effect ('It's all here') or vocabulary to persuade ('perfect gateway', 'renowned restaurants'). However, you need to remember that it is the quality of the comments you make on the features, not the number of features you identify, that gains you high marks. It is much better to say a lot about three features than a little about five.

Evaluating effectiveness

In an exam you may be asked to evaluate the effectiveness of the presentation and/or language of a text. This means that you need to make a series of judgements on how successful it is. In order to do this, you need first to think carefully about its **intended purpose(s)** and **audience(s)**.

Key terms

Intended purpose: the reason or reasons for which a text is produced.

Intended audience: the reader or readers for whom the text is written.

8 Which of the following purposes is appropriate to the Seattle advertisement? Give reasons based on the text to support your selection.

- To inform the reader about Seattle.
- To advise the reader about what to do in Seattle.
- To persuade the reader to go to Seattle.
- To persuade the reader to find out more about Seattle.
- To advertise Seattle as a tourist destination.

9 Place your selected purposes in rank order with the most important purpose first.

10 Which of the following audiences is targeted by the Seattle advertisement? Give reasons based on the text to support your selection.

- People who want a quiet holiday.
- People who intend to visit the Pacific Northwest.
- People seeking a holiday in the US.
- People who want a holiday that offers a range of activities.
- People interested in setting up a business in Seattle.

11 Place your selected audiences in rank order with the most clearly targeted audience first.

In any answer in which you evaluate a text, you need to show you have thought about:

- how well it achieves its intended purpose(s)
- how well it targets its intended audience(s).

The following question focuses on both use of language and presentational features:

- How do the headline and the picture add to the effectiveness of the text?

Read one student's A* answer to this question. The different skills that the student shows are annotated for you.

Shows awareness of structure

Shows understanding of structure

Comments on effect

Shows understanding of structure

Embedded quotation

Interprets image

Refers to intended audience

Original inference

Makes judgement

Embedded quotation

Refers to purpose

Refers to intended audience

> The headline is set prominently in large uppercase font at the top of the advert. The first word, Seattle, immediately tells you the main subject of the text. The white font is set against the pale blue background of the sky making the words look almost cloud-like and providing a strong contrast with the dark blue background at the bottom – perhaps framing the advert with a suggestion of day and night. This is reinforced by the photograph of Seattle, placed centrally for maximum effect. Although the lights are on, it is not clear whether it is sunrise or sunset, suggesting that this is an exciting city where something is happening at all hours of day and night. The city is set against a backdrop of a mountain, which links with the word 'gateway' in the headline. It is as though you need to move through the city to get to the mountain. Both places appear to offer the opportunity for 'adventure', and would appeal to tourists looking for something different. The focus on the famous landmark of the Space Tower, where Meg Ryan met Tom Hanks at the end of 'Sleepless in Seattle', adds a touch of romance for those who know the film.
>   The combination of headline and photograph is very effective in giving a visual illustration of the 'urban and natural', which is referred to later. They reinforce the purpose of the advert, which is to attract visitors to Seattle. Many adults thinking about a holiday would be attracted by this, the muted light of the sky combined with the city lights making Seattle seem both mysterious and, at the same time, lively – the kind of place you would want to visit.

Links to other part of text

Shows understanding of structure

Uses discursive marker to link ideas

Interprets image

Links picture and headline

Makes judgement

Links to other part of text

Justifies judgement with reference to purpose

Practice question

4 How do the words written under the photograph (from 'Seattle' to 'local representative') add to the effectiveness of the text?

Remember to:

- show awareness of intended purpose and audience
- show skills of inference, deduction and interpretation
- make judgements supported by evidence.

Check your revision

You are now going to find out how well you have understood the work in this chapter. On the opposite page you will see another advertisement similar to the one you have studied in detail.

Read Item 1.2, the advertisement called 'Washington State: green before green was cool', and complete the following tasks using the prompts to help you.

Reading with understanding

What does the advert suggest a visitor can do in Washington State?

Remember:

- if you simply list literal details you will not get high marks. You need to show that you are able to work out what is being 'suggested' or implied by the advertisement
- you need to 'offer relevant and appropriate quotation' to support your comments.

Commenting on structure and presentation

Write a paragraph about the use of colour in the advertisement.

Remember:

- you need to show skills of inference, interpretation and deduction
- you should refer to details in the text to support your comments.

Thinking about language

Write a detailed comment on the use of adjectives in the text.

Remember:

- you need to show that you can analyse use of language
- you should write a lot about a little.

Evaluating effectiveness

How do the structure and presentation of this advertisement add to its effectiveness? Remember to:

- first identify the intended purpose(s) and audience(s)
- make judgements on effectiveness
- support your judgements with references to details in the text
- show skills of inference, deduction and interpretation
- include any original ideas you may have.

Assessment

Look back through your answers. Highlight in one colour comments you have made that show inference, deduction and/or interpretation. Use another colour to highlight references to details in the text and/or embedded quotations. Use a third colour to highlight any original observations you have made.

Item 1.2

HOH RAINFOREST, OLYMPIC NATIONAL PARK.

WASHINGTON STATE:
GREEN BEFORE GREEN WAS COOL.

Photo: Rachel_TheCat

Less than 100 miles from the urban metropolis of Seattle lies a mystical world. Lush, green, quiet, moss-covered, fresh-scented, the Hoh Rain Forest is a "must see" for any world traveler. The Hoh and the Quinault Rain Forests, both located in Washington's Olympic National Park, are just two of the reasons that the Olympic National Park has been named a UNESCO World Heritage Site and an International Biosphere Reserve.

Here you can walk, hike, bike, raft or kayak through primeval forests, experience mineral-rich hot springs, or enjoy 70 miles of rugged coastline.

The Olympic National Park...just one of the boundless discoveries you will find in Washington, the state.

To begin your journey, please visit www.ExperienceWA.com

Or contact our local representatives:

ExperienceWA.com
Washington State Tourism

In the United Kingdom:
First Public Relations
Tel: +44 (20) 7978 5233
Fax: +44 (20) 7924 3134
web: www.firstpr.co.uk

In Belgium, Netherlands and Luxembourg:
BuroSix
Tel: +31 (0) 182 39 44 55
Fax: +31 (0) 654 28 03 32
info@burosix.nl
www.burosix.nl

Reading reviews

Exploring meaning

In your English examination you may be asked to write about the ideas contained within a text and/or the ways those ideas are expressed and presented.

There may be words that you do not understand in the Items you are given to read. You will not be able to use a dictionary, but you will nearly always be able to work out the general meaning of a word by:

- thinking about words you do know that may be connected with it
- looking at the context in which the word is placed.

Objectives

In this chapter you will revise:

exploring meaning and tone

investigating how language is used

commenting on structure and presentation

evaluating effectiveness.

Activity

1 Read Item 2.1, which is a book review. As you read it, list any words or phrases where you are puzzled by the meaning or the usage.

Item 2.1

True tribal style

Venture into the mysterious world of Ethiopia's Surma and Mursi tribes with this striking book of portraits.

Dawn breaks in Ethiopia's isolated Omo Valley. For the tribespeople it's another typical day: collecting water, herding goats and … getting dressed up.

Life here can be bleak; the arms and ivory trades flourish and guerrilla warfare is commonplace. But all this is punctuated by rather more innocent pursuits. Just for the fun of it, the Omo's men, women and kids indulge in a daily, centuries-old rhythm of fancy dress. And we're not talking a half-hearted effort either: when it comes to costumes, make-up and elaborate headgear, the Omo tribes really go to town.

Photographer Hans Silvester has journeyed to their homeland 12 times. His latest tome is bursting with dazzling portraits showcasing their penchant for body adornment. The shots reveal theatrical headdresses fashioned out of banana leaves, necklaces made of snail shells and naked limbs smeared with volcanic body paint.

Other more unsettling get-ups involve monkey skins, butterfly wings and lip disks – women create painful holes in their lower lip and insert round plates, thus increasing their chances of snagging a rich husband.

The book doesn't offer an intimate peek inside the tribes' daily lives. Indeed, some of the portraits look so exquisitely styled they smack of a *Vogue* photo shoot, leaving you wondering if it's all just a contrived show for the camera. But this is an intrinsic part of their culture, and would continue regardless of whether our eyes were on them.

'Body painting, as practised here in east Africa, the cradle of humanity, … represents a way of life that dates from prehistory,' muses Silvester. 'Perhaps underlying it all is the spirit of the hunter, accustomed to camouflage … or perhaps it is simply and unconscious homage to Mother Earth.'

Whatever drives the Omo people to get kitted out in their finery, it's impossible not to marvel at the visual spectacle. You'll be entranced by this striking record of a fascinating but increasingly fragile community. **Anna Webber**

Natural Fashion, Hans Silvester (Thames & Hudson, £18.95)

You may have listed the word 'punctuated', not because you have not come across it before but because you usually think about punctuation in terms of writing skills. Using what you know about the word and then thinking about its context will help you to understand its meaning in the sentence:

Punctuation gives pausing and sense to writing. Here, 'punctuated' suggests that the bleakness of the life is broken up or given sense by the more 'innocent pursuits'.

But all this is **punctuated** by rather more innocent pursuits.

Now look at the following sentence. It contains three words that may cause problems for you. The annotations show how you could work out meaning:

Connects with 'His latest'. As this is a book review, it is reasonable to guess that a tome is a book. The word usually suggests a large, weighty book.

A showcase is used to display objects so that they look good. Here the word suggests that the portraits show the body adornment in a good light.

His latest **tome** is bursting with dazzling portraits **showcasing** their **penchant** for body adornment.

This is linked with 'their' and 'body adornment'. We already know that these people are enthusiastic about body adornment and can guess, correctly, that the word means a liking for this.

Activity

2 Look back at the list you made in Activity 1. Try to work out the meaning of the words you have listed using:

- what you already know about them
- what you can work out from the context.

When you have done this you may want to check their meaning in a dictionary.

Top Tip

Never be put off by words you do not at first understand. Make an intelligent guess at their meaning. You will not lose marks for not knowing the meaning of the occasional word.

Thinking about tone

Writers often choose a particular tone with which to write. This may, for example, be friendly, angry, sarcastic, humorous, or any combination of these. If you can work out the tone, then you have vital clues regarding the writer's attitude to the subject about which they are writing and sometimes their attitude to the reader.

3 Read the following sentences and, for each one, select one or more words from the list below to describe the tone adopted by the writer.

a And we're not talking a half-hearted effort either: when it comes to costumes, make-up and elaborate headgear, the Omo tribes really go to town.

b His latest tome is bursting with dazzling portraits showcasing their penchant for body adornment.

c Other more unsettling get-ups involve monkey skins, butterfly wings and lip disks – women create painful holes in their lower lip and insert round plates, thus increasing their chances of snagging a rich husband.

d Indeed, some of the portraits look so exquisitely styled they smack of a Vogue photo shoot.

e Whatever drives the Omo people to get kitted out in their finery, it's impossible not to marvel at the visual spectacle.

f You'll be entranced by this striking record of a fascinating but increasingly fragile community.

informal   sarcastic   amused   affectionate   serious

humorous   concerned   critical   cynical   enthusiastic

4 As you can see, the tone can change within a text. Use what you have worked out about tone to help you write one sentence about each of the following:

a the writer's attitude to his reader

b the writer's attitude to the book he is reviewing

c the writer's attitude to the Omo tribes.

Investigating language

When answering a question about the writer's use of language, you need to look for a few distinctive features to write about in detail rather than trying to say a little about everything. Your aim is to show:

- you can examine the use of language
- you can work out things about the writer's intended purpose.

5 In the following example, the student:

a examines how the writer builds a relationship with the reader

b comments on the writer's purpose.

Highlight the points about language in one colour and the comments on purpose in another colour.

> The subheading starts with the directive 'Venture into'. Here the writer immediately addresses the reader directly and the word 'venture' with its echoes of 'adventure' suggests this might be an exciting thing to do. Personal pronouns are used to involve the reader and anticipate his or her likely response to the book: 'leaving you wondering'; 'you'll be entranced by'. This helps to make the writing feel personal to the specific reader rather than the general public. Added to this the writer uses pronouns to put herself on the same side as the reader: 'And we're not talking ...'; 'our eyes'. By doing this the intention is to draw the reader in and make the reader feel as though the writer understands his or her needs and has similar ones.

Activity

6   The use of lists is a specific language device. Complete the following stages to help you write a paragraph in which you examine the use of lists in this review.

   a   Find examples of lists and think about how each one is being used.

   b   Make a note of the different things you can say about the lists themselves, how they are presented and the intended effect on the reader.

   c   Write your paragraph remembering to show you can:

      i   examine the use of language

      ii   work out things about the writer's intended purpose.

Commenting on structure and presentation

The visual features of this review are fairly obvious and easy to comment on. A range of font sizes is used. As would be expected, the title is presented in the largest font and the main body of text is in the smallest font. There is perhaps more you could say about the photographs and their positioning within the review.

Activity

7   Write a paragraph about the photographs and their use in this review. It will help you to first think about and make notes on:

   a   the positioning of the photographs on the page

   b   what the photographs reveal to the reader

   c   the connection between the photographs and the written text.

   Remember to show your higher-level reading skills of inference, interpretation and deduction when writing your paragraph.

Below is one student's paragraph about the use of photographs in the review. The comments that reveal high-level reading skills are highlighted for you. Look again at your answer and highlight the parts that reveal high-level reading skills. Compare your answer with the student's answer and decide which one is best.

> Photographs are taken from the book being reviewed to act as illustration of what is being described in the written text. Presumably they were selected to intrigue the readers and to in some way challenge them, as the gaze of the subject in each photo is directed at the reader. The expression on each face is serious. This particular selection of photographs suggests to the reader that this is not something to be ridiculed or taken lightly, and also hints at the fragility referred to in the final sentence. The larger photograph has a visual dominance in the article whilst the second one is placed centrally in the written text though, interestingly, the larger photograph could be cut without damaging the review as a whole. It is an additional illustration, rather than an essential one.

Top Tip

It is not enough to identify features of presentation. You need to show you can infer, interpret and deduce meaning from these features.

There is more to structure than just the visual features. You also need to consider how the written text of the review has been constructed.

Activity

8 Answer the following questions to help you understand the structure of the written text.

a How does the headline reflect the content of the review? At what stage of reading the review does the meaning of the headline become clear?

b At what point do you realise that this is a book review?

c An examination of the contents of each paragraph will lead to a better understanding of how the review is constructed. Match the paragraph numbers (1–7) to the appropriate summary of content below (a–g).

Paragraph 1   a makes first reference to the book outside the sub-heading

Paragraph 2   b develops points by revealing concerns

Paragraph 3   c uses quotation from the book's author

Paragraph 4   d summarises expected reader response to the book

Paragraph 5   e reveals an intriguing point which 'hooks' the reader

Paragraph 6   f includes potential criticisms of the book

Paragraph 7   g explains the point made in the opening paragraph

Evaluating effectiveness

In an exam you may be asked to evaluate the effectiveness of the presentation and/or the language of a text. This means that you need to make a series of judgements about how successful it is. To do this, you need first to think carefully about its intended purpose and audience.

Remember, a text may have more than one intended purpose and intended audience.

In any answer in which you evaluate a text, you need to show you have thought about:

- how well it achieves its intended purpose(s)
- how well it targets its intended audience(s).

Top Tip

When evaluating a text, remember that it is not simply a case of whether you personally find it effective; you may not be the intended audience.

Activity

9 Which of the following purposes is appropriate to this review? Give reasons based on the text to support your selection.

a To inform the reader about the Omo people.

b To inform the reader about the book *Natural Fashion*.

c To advise the reader to read a particular book.

d To advise the reader not to read a particular book.

e To reveal the writer's opinion of a particular book.

Place your selected purposes in rank order with the most important purpose first.

10 Which of the following audiences is targeted by the review? Give reasons based on the text to support your selection.

a School students interested in art and photography.

b Adults who want to learn about Ethiopia.

c Adults interested in art and photography.

d People interested in learning about other cultures.

Place your selected audiences in rank order with the most clearly targeted audience first.

Sample question and answer

The following question focuses on the use of language in the review:

> How effective is the writer's use of language in this review?

Read one student's answer to this question. The features of the answer are annotated for you.

Shows awareness of purpose

Close examination of technique

The writer attracts the reader's attention immediately through the clever use of sound to link the three words in the headline: 'True tribal style'. The 'tr' sound occurs at the beginning of the first and second word with the 't' sound appearing again after the 's' in style. There is also the 'i' in tribal and the 'y' in style and the 'l' in tribal and the 'l' in style. So the words are connected by sound as well as by meaning and have a neat effective ring to them.

Assesses effect

Infers meaning

From the outset, the writer speaks directly to the reader, starting with the directive to 'venture into' with its connotations of adventure, and followed by the use of a series of personal pronouns. The word 'you' as in 'leaving you wondering' and 'you'll be entranced by' targets each reader as an individual. It anticipates a precise (and positive) response and creates a personal and friendly tone.

Understands purpose

Understands purpose

Assesses effect

Uses discursive marker to link ideas

In addition to this the writer uses pronouns to put herself on the same side as the reader: 'And we're not talking …'; 'our eyes'. By doing this the intention is to draw the reader in and this simple technique is likely to make the reader feel as though the writer understands his or her needs and has similar ones.

Understands purpose

Evaluates effectiveness

The vocabulary in the review is adult and sophisticated, for example 'warfare is commonplace'; 'an intrinsic part of their culture'. The audience of such a review is likely to be adult and one that is interested in art and other cultures. Such sophisticated use of language is entirely appropriate for such an audience and would be likely to engage and sustain their attention.

Refers to intended audience

Supports comment with textual detail

Evaluates likely effectiveness on intended audience

Practice question

1 Look back on the work you have done on presentation and structure in this chapter before writing an answer to this question:

> Comment on the effectiveness of the structure and presentation of this review.

Remember to:
- show awareness of intended purpose and audience
- show skills of inference, deduction and interpretation
- consider how the ideas are structured as well as the visual structure.

Check your revision

You are now going to find out how well you have understood the work in this chapter. Below you will see another review that bears some similarities to the one you have studied in detail.

Read Item 2.2, the review of Tony Hawk Ride, and complete the following tasks. Use the prompts to help you.

Exploring meaning

Find the following extracts in the article. Work out the meaning of the underlined word in each extract.

> 'The result: half-functioning hardware that fails to function with consistency and a shallow game <u>devoid</u> of excitement.'

> 'It also feels weighty and <u>resilient</u>, as if ready to withstand hours of punishment.'

> 'This is partially because … though it's hard to take it seriously as a sim when you <u>inadvertently</u> skate across the ceiling or happen upon pedestrians…'

Remember:

- use your current knowledge
- use what you learn from the context in which the word is used.

Thinking about tone

Which of the following words best describe the tone adopted by the writer in this review? Support each choice with an example from the review.

informal   sarcastic   amused   affectionate   serious   friendly   excited

humorous   concerned   critical   cynical   enthusiastic   patronising

Remember:

- The writer's tone can change from one part of a text to another.
- You need to 'offer relevant and appropriate quotation' to support your comments.

Investigating language

Write a detailed comment on the use of repetition in the final paragraph of this review.

Remember to show that you can:

- examine and analyse use of language
- work out things about the writer's intended purpose.

Commenting on structure and presentation

Write a paragraph about the way this review is structured.

Remember:

- You need to comment on how the review is set out on the page and how the written text is organised and developed.
- You need to show skills of inference, interpretation and deduction.

Evaluating effectiveness

How effective is the writer's use of language in this review?

Remember to:

- first identify the intended purpose(s) and audience(s)
- make judgements on effectiveness
- support your judgements with references to details of the text
- show skills of inference, deduction and interpretation
- include any original ideas that you may have.

Assessment

Look back through your answers. Highlight comments you have made that show inference, deduction and/or interpretation in one colour. Use another colour to highlight references to details in the text and/or embedded quotations. Use a third colour to highlight any original observations you have made.

Tony Hawk Ride

* Activision
* Robomodo
* Skateboarding
* Release: Dec 4, 2009 »
* PEGI:

Also on **More Info**

X360 WII

Summary

Reviews
  GameSpot Review ›
  Player Reviews
  Critic Scores

News

Previews & Features

Images

Videos

Answers

Hints & Cheats

Forum

Games you may like...

Hawk's Proving Ground (PS3)

Tony Hawk's Project 8 (PS3)

Skate (PS3)

Skate 2 (PS3)

⊞ Add Game | 🏷 Tag | 🖶 Print | ✉ Email | f Facebook | 🗞 Digg | ⓔ Tweet

Tony Hawk Ride Review

Busted controls and stripped-down gameplay make Tony Hawk Ride an overpriced fiasco.

The Good

The included skateboard peripheral is durable.

The Bad

Movements don't register correctly much of the time ● Bad menu organization and other presentation issues ● Challenge mode stinks, and every mode is stripped ● Tiny skating areas ● Really expensive.

Tony Hawk Ride is the ultimate triumph of gimmick over game. The concept: build a skateboard peripheral that lets players simulate skateboarding in their living rooms. The result: half-functioning hardware that fails to function with consistency and a shallow game devoid of excitement. Vert skating and free skating are the only sources of mild enjoyment here, but the fun is too short lived to justify the whopping $120 price tag.

It's impossible to separate the board from the game. After all, Tony Hawk Ride must be played with the included skateboard peripheral. It takes some time to get used to the feel of the board, though your skating career begins with a number of tutorials that help you get on your feet, so to speak. From there, it's a matter of completing races, performing tricks for points, and nailing short challenges as you trudge your way through Ride's single-player experience. Fortunately, the peripheral is easy to set up and physically solid. It also feels weighty and resilient, as if ready to withstand hours of punishment.

Yet while the hardware can take a beating, the oft-useless board all too often fails to read your movements with the precision necessary for the game to deliver any amount of fun. Manuals, ollies, and nollies are relatively simple to pull off. You perform manuals much as you'd expect: by raising the nose or tail of the board in the air and holding the position. You do ollies by popping the nose into the air, while nollies, of course, are executed by popping up the tail. But, when Tony Hawk Ride starts expecting you to pull off anything more precise, it collapses.

Tricks that involve the infrared sensors on the front, back, and sides of the peripheral are arbitrary, working only some of the time. You swipe or hover your hand over these sensors when you want to perform finger flips and grabs. But these moves aren't consistent. If you fail the trick, you're never sure whether you swiped your hand across the sensor too early, held it there too long, or your movement wasn't recognized at all.

Tony Hawk Ride's flaws don't end with the lousy controls. The game feels half finished, offering up the most bare-bones experience possible. Don't expect skater-specific specials or large, high-concept levels. You can free skate, but most of the areas are small and none of them offer the fast-paced freewheeling of previous Tony Hawk games. This is partially because Ride seems to fancy itself a simulation, though it's hard to take it seriously as a sim when you inadvertently skate across the ceiling or happen upon pedestrians that exclaim their surprise when you almost run into them…in the middle of a skate park.

You see Tony Hawk Ride's shallowness everywhere. You see it in its bare-bones online modes, which very few people are playing. You see it in the visuals, which get the job done without a lick of energy or personality. And you see it every time you have to endure the rest of the challenge, even if you're bound to replay it because you failed the first trick. Tony Hawk Ride is a waste of money.

By Kevin VanOrd, GameSpot Posted Dec 4, 2009 12:12 am GMT

GameSpot Score	Critic Score 22 reviews	4.9
3.5 bad	User Score 110 votes	4.3
	Your Score slide to rate	N/A

About the rating system »   **Review the Game**

Game Emblems

The Bad

the-dude12
Tony Hawk Ride is a good fun game for the whole family.
Continue »

Ⓖ **8.0** great

Jack_n_Coke07
Awesome idea, really odd execution.....but still keeps you playing
Continue »

6.5 fair

Critic Scores	See All
PSX Extreme	4 / 10
IGN	5 / 10
VideoGamer	4 / 10
1UP	D+
Gamervision	5.5 / 10
GameZone	9.2 / 10
NZGamer	4.5 / 10
GamingExcellence	4 / 10

*The links above will take you to other Web sites and are provided for your reference. GameSpot does not produce or endorse the content on these sites.

CBS Interactive Inc., www.gamespot.com/ps3/sports/tonyhawkride/review.html

Objectives

In this chapter you will revise:

selecting and using material from different texts

pointing out similarities and differences between texts

writing a comparison.

Making comparisons

What is the question?

In your English examination you will be asked to compare two texts. You do not need to compare every aspect of the texts. You will be given a specific area on which to focus. For example:

> Compare the ways in which presentational features are used for effect in the two texts. Examine some examples and explain what the effects are.

This question can be broken down to highlight the different things you need to do:

Point out similarities and differences

Focus on techniques

Write about use of colour, illustrations, etc.

Consider how they are used to influence the audience and achieve purpose

Compare the ways in which presentational features are used for effect in Item 1 and Item 2. Examine some examples and explain what their effects are.

Write about these two items only

Focus on a few (3–5) features – do not try to write about everything

Show you can analyse

Make evaluative judgements

Whatever the focus of the question, you will always be required to write about the techniques. The question may refer to 'the ways', 'the techniques', 'the methods', or sometimes it may ask 'How does …?' These are the signpost words that tell you that you must write about the techniques.

Practice question

1 Using the example above as a model, highlight and annotate each of the following examination questions to show you understand what you are being asked to do:

- How is language used for effect in Item 1? Compare this with the way language is used for effect in Item 2. Examine some examples from both items and explain what their effects are.

- Compare the methods used in Item 1 and Item 2 to make the text appeal to the reader. Examine some examples and explain what the effects are.

- Compare how language is used to influence the intended audience in Item 1 and Item 2. Examine some examples and explain what the effects are.

- Examine some examples of the ways in which presentational and structural devices are used for effect in Item 1. Compare these with examples of how presentational and structural devices are used for effect in Item 2.

The skills you need to show 🔊

In your exam you need to select relevant points from the two texts and to compare them. Here are some of the words and phrases you can use to help you make comparisons:

however	although	in the same way as	similarly
differently	and	more	less
in contrast with	contrastingly	alternatively	both
neither	but	also	this differs from

While the language of comparison will help you, it is, as always, the quality of the comments you make that will gain you high marks. You need to demonstrate high-level reading skills and show your ability to:

- analyse detail
- explore meaning
- demonstrate understanding of purpose and audience
- evaluate effectiveness.

Look again at Item 1.1 on page 3 and Item 2.1 on page 10, and remind yourself of the work you have done on them.

> **Top Tip**
>
> Learning the language of comparison will help you to express your ideas. However, it is the quality of the comments that you make which will gain you high marks.

SEATTLE: GATEWAY TO YOUR WASHINGTON STATE ADVENTURE.

Seattle: the perfect mix of experiences. Cosmopolitan and casual. Industrious and playful. High-tech and hand-crafted. Urban and natural.

With over 25 international flights arriving regularly, Seattle is the perfect gateway to begin your exploration of Washington, and the Pacific Northwest.

Experience the city's renowned restaurants, shops and cultural attractions. Take a day trip to nearby islands. Jump on a ferry to the mountains or the rainforests, or journey east to the high desert and wine regions. It's all here.

Oh, and we also make a pretty good cup of coffee.

To begin your journey, please visit www.ExperienceWA.com

Or contact our local representative:

ExperienceWA.com
Washington State Tourism

In the United Kingdom:
First Public Relations
Tel: +44 (20) 7978 5233
Fax: +44 (20) 7924 3134
web: www.firstpr.co.uk

In Belgium, Netherlands and Luxembourg:
BuroSix
Tel: +31 (0) 182 39 44 55
Fax: +31 (0) 654 28 03 32
info@burosix.nl
www.burosix.nl

True tribal style

Venture into the mysterious world of Ethiopia's Surma and Mursi tribes with this striking book of portraits.

Dawn breaks in Ethiopia's isolated Omo Valley. For the tribespeople it's another typical day: collecting water, herding goats and ... getting dressed up.

Life here can be bleak; the arms and ivory trades flourish and guerrilla warfare is commonplace. But all this is punctuated by rather more innocent pursuits. Just for the fun of it, the Omo's men, women and kids indulge in a daily, centuries-old rhythm of fancy dress. And we're not talking a half-hearted effort either: when it comes to costumes, make-up and elaborate headgear, the Omo tribes really go to town.

Photographer Hans Silvester has journeyed to their homeland 12 times. His latest tome is bursting with dazzling portraits showcasing their penchant for body adornment. The shots reveal theatrical headdresses fashioned out of banana leaves, necklaces made of snail shells and naked limbs smeared with volcanic body paint.

Other more unsettling get-ups involve monkey skins, butterfly wings and lip disks – women create painful holes in their lower lip and insert round plates, thus increasing their chances of snagging a rich husband.

The book doesn't offer an intimate peek inside the tribes' daily lives. Indeed, some of the portraits look so exquisitely styled they smack of a *Vogue* photo shoot, leaving you wondering if it's all just a contrived show for the camera. But this is an intrinsic part of their culture, and would continue regardless of whether our eyes were on them.

'Body painting, as practised here in east Africa, the cradle of humanity, ... represents a way of life that dates from prehistory,' muses Silvester. 'Perhaps underlying it all is the spirit of the hunter, accustomed to camouflage ... or perhaps it is simply and unconscious homage to Mother Earth.'

Whatever drives the Omo people to get kitted out in their finery, it's impossible not to marvel at the visual spectacle. You'll be entranced by this striking record of a fascinating but increasingly fragile community.
Anna Webber

Natural Fashion, Hans Silvester (Thames & Hudson, £18.95)

Now read the following extracts from two students' answers to the question you examined earlier.

Sample question and answer

Compare the ways in which presentational features are used for effect in the two Items above. Examine some examples and explain what their effects are.

The language of comparison is highlighted in both extracts and the annotations show you the examiner's comments.

Example 1

Pictures are used in both Item 1.1 and Item 2.1. In Item 1.1 there is a photograph of Seattle whereas in Item 2.1 there are two photographs of tribal women. The photograph of Seattle shows you the city with all the lights on to make it look like an interesting place to go to. However, the photographs of the two women show you them in their costumes. This is also done to make it look interesting. In both Items the photographs are large so that the reader can see them clearly. In Item 1.1 the photograph is placed centrally with the title above it and the rest of the writing below it. It is different in Item 2.1 where there are two photographs. One is placed above the main writing and the other is placed in the middle of it. Both Items use photographs effectively but I prefer the photograph used in Item 1.1 as it makes me feel I would like to go to Seattle.

Annotations (left): Refers to detail; Awareness of purpose; Makes a simple point of similarity; Awareness of structure; Refers to detail; Gives personal response

Annotations (right): Simple link; Simple explanation of link; Refers to detail; Makes a point of similarity; Makes a simple point of difference; Makes a point of similarity

Example 2

The centrally placed photograph of Seattle with its background of mountains effectively illustrates for the reader the contrast between 'urban and natural' laid claim to in the written text. The sparkling lights, combined with the suggestion that this could be either dawn or dusk, create the impression of a lively city and, like New York, one that never sleeps. The photographs in Item 2.1, one placed centrally as in Item 1.1, have also been used as illustration, in this case to show examples of what you will see if you buy the book. They have, presumably, been carefully selected to intrigue the reader, demonstrating as they do the fragility of these people and also containing, in the direction of the eyes to the reader, a kind of challenge to discover more about them. In both texts the photographs are likely to initially engage and interest the reader and to enhance the written content.

Annotations (left): Refers to detail; Shows close attention to detail; Explains effect; Makes point of similarity; Understands purpose; Compares effectiveness

Annotations (right): Aware of structure; Links photograph with written text and shows understanding of purpose; Explores meaning; Compares purpose; Exploration and inference; Analysis of illustration

Did you notice that although the second example uses less language of comparison, it contains far more evidence of high-level reading skills (understanding, exploration, inference and analysis) and would gain a much higher mark than the first example?

Practice question

2 Below are other points made by the student who wrote Example 1. Rewrite them aiming to demonstrate high-level reading skills. For each one you are given a prompt (in italic) to help develop your thinking.

> *Although they use different colours, the illustrations in both Item 1.1 and Item 2.1 are colourful to make them stand out and catch the attention of the reader.*

Can you say anything specific about the colours and the things you associate with them?

How is the information revealed to you in both Items? Why is it revealed in this way? Is it effective?

> *The items are structured very differently as one is an advertisement and the other is a book review. Item 1.1 is organised into four distinct sections whereas Item 2.1 has the main picture and then the rest of the article.*

Are there any significant features of the fonts that have been used? Are there similarities in when the largest and smallest fonts are used?

> *A range of fonts is used in both Items.*

Making choices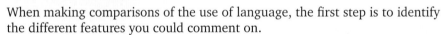

When making comparisons of the use of language, the first step is to identify the different features you could comment on.

Activity

1 The following chart identifies some particular uses of language in Items 1.1 and 2.1. Copy and complete the chart by identifying two more examples of each feature.

Feature of language use in Item 1.1	Example(s) of feature	Feature of language use in Item 2.1	Example(s) of feature
Phrases containing contrasts	'cosmopolitan and casual'	Addresses reader directly	'leaving you wondering'
Addresses reader directly	'your Washington State adventure'	Lists	'collecting water, herding goats and … getting dressed up'
Directives	'experience'	Sophisticated vocabulary	'guerrilla warfare is commonplace'
Present tense	'Seattle is'	Vocabulary to persuade	'dazzling portraits'
Vocabulary to persuade	'perfect gateway'	Present tense	'Dawn breaks'

In an exam you do not have time to compare everything. Aim to select the features that allow you to comment in detail and show high-level skills.

Writing an answer

Many students have lots of good ideas about the use of language. They sometimes find it difficult to put these into writing in an exam. The trick is to know exactly what is expected of you before you go into your exam, and to practise.

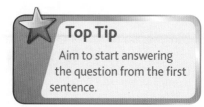

Top Tip

Aim to start answering the question from the first sentence.

Activity

2 Below are the first two paragraphs of one student's answer to the following question:

> Compare the ways language used for effect in Item 1.1 (page 3)? Compare this with the way language is used for effect in Item 2.1 (page 10). Examine some examples from both Items and explain what their effects are.

Read the student response and highlight or annotate where they:

a demonstrate skills of exploration, inference and analysis

b point out similarities and differences

c refer to the text to support the points they make

d show understanding of intended purpose and/or audience.

> The writers of both texts share a technique in common: they both address the reader directly through the use of directives and personal pronouns. In Item 1.1 the reader is directed to 'experience', 'jump', 'take' and 'journey'. These verbs all suggest action and movement, successfully reinforcing the notion that there is much to do in Seattle and mirroring the implication of the earlier phrase 'industrious and playful'. The writer of Item 2.1 makes more limited use of directives though the one that is used is placed in a strategic position. At the start of the sub-heading the reader is directed to 'Venture into', the word 'venture' with its echoes of 'adventure' suggests this will be an exciting thing to do.
>
> Personal pronouns are used by both writers. Item 1.1 writer refers to 'your Washington State adventure', 'your journey', targeting the reader and making them feel as though the text is personally directed to them. Similarly, in Item 2.1 we find 'leaving you wondering' and 'you'll be entranced by', whereby the writer raises the reader's expectations and anticipates his or her response. Added to this the writer uses pronouns to place herself on the same side as the reader: 'And we're not talking ...'; 'our eyes', making the reader feel as though the writer understands his or her needs and has similar ones. This differs slightly from the use of the first person plural in Item 1.1 where there is a clearer distinction between the reader and the writer with the writer belonging to the 'we' who makes the coffee, emphasising how the firm is there to serve the customer.

Practice question

3 Write another paragraph that could form part of this response. Choose carefully from your chart and make sure you have plenty to say before you start to write. The sections on language in Chapters 1 and 2 may help you. Remember to:

- demonstrate skills of exploration, inference and analysis
- point out similarities and differences
- refer to the text to support the points you make
- evaluate the effect on purpose and audience.

Check your revision

You are now going to find out how well you have understood the work in this chapter. Look again at Item 1.2 (page 9), 'Washington State: green before green was cool', and Item 2.2 (page 17), Tony Hawk Ride, and remind yourself of the work you have done on these.

What is the question?

Highlight and annotate each of the following examination questions to show you understand what you are being asked to do:

> Compare how language is used for effect in Item 1.2 and Item 2.2. Examine some examples from both Items and explain what their effects are.

> Compare the ways in which presentational devices are used to make the subject seem appealing in Item 1.2 and Item 2.2. Examine some examples and evaluate their effectiveness.

The skills you need to show

- List 10 words or phrases that you could use to help you make comparisons between features of texts.
- Which high-level reading skills do you need to demonstrate in your comparison?
- Write a paragraph comparing the use of illustrations in Item 1.2 and Item 2.2. Highlight the words you have used to point out similarities and/or differences.

Making choices

Make a chart similar to that on page 21, in which you list the main features of the use of language in Item 1.2 and Item 2.2 and examples of these features.

Choose two or three features from each Item that you think are particularly significant. For each one, list points you could make that would show high-level reading skills.

Writing an answer

Compare how language is used for effect in Item 1.2 and Item 2.2. Examine some examples from both Items and explain what their effects are.

Remember to:

- demonstrate skills of exploration, inference and analysis
- point out similarities and differences
- refer to the text to support the points you make
- show understanding of intended purpose and audience.

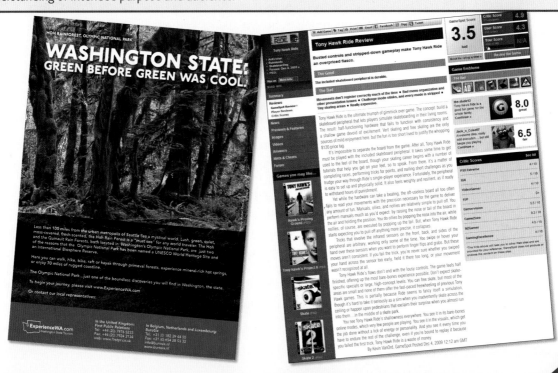

4

Key terms

Chronological order: the order in which something happens.

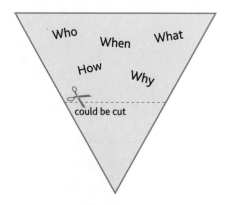

Non-fiction prose

Structure

Structure is to do with order, i.e. the order in which information is revealed to you. One common form of structure is chronological order – the order in which things happen or happened. Many stories are told in chronological order. A fairy story, for example, usually starts with 'Once upon a time …', proceeds to tell the story of events in the order in which they occurred and ends with 'they all lived happily ever after'. A chronological story is easy to follow and this makes it suitable for young children. Recipes are also written in **chronological order** – if not, the meal would be a disaster.

How a piece of writing is structured will depend largely on its purpose, audience and context.

Examining the structure of newspaper articles

Journalists use a variety of structures for writing their news stories. One of the most common of these is the 'inverted pyramid' structure where journalists sum up the most important news first: Who? What? Where? When? Why? How? Less-important information is added later. There are two main reasons for this:

- Readers are often in a hurry. They want the main details and will then decide whether to read the full story. The main details act as a 'hook' to draw them in.
- Journalists do not always know how much space will be available for their story. Giving the essential details at the start enables the editor to cut the story at a later stage.

Activity

1 Read Item 4.1, a news article.

   a Decide at which stage the essential questions (Who? What? Where? When? Why? How?) have been answered.

   b At what point does the meaning of the term 'homeopathy' used in the headline become clear in the article? What does this suggest to you about the journalist's assumptions about his reader?

   c The article is written in tabloid paragraphs, many of which contain one sentence and the longest of which is three sentences. Suggest two reasons for this that are linked with purpose, audience or context.

Item 4.1

'Mass overdose' homeopathy protest at Boots

Sam Jones

Hundreds of sceptics will stage a 'mass overdose' outside Boots stores around Britain today to protest against the chain's continuing sale of homeopathic remedies and to argue that such treatments have no scientific basis.

The event will see the protesters swallow entire bottles of homeopathic pills to illustrate their claims that such remedies 'are nothing but sugar pills'.

It is being co-ordinated by the Merseyside Skeptics Society, a non-profit organisation dedicated to 'developing and supporting the sceptical community'. It will take place outside Boots stores in Birmingham, Brighton, Edinburgh, Glasgow, Hampshire, Leeds, Leicester, London, Liverpool, Manchester, Oxford and Sheffield. 'Sympathy events' will also be held in Canada and Australia.

Homeopathy, which uses highly diluted substances to trigger healing, was developed by the German physician Samuel Hahnemann in the late 18th century. Homeopaths say water retains a memory of the substance, which has a therapeutic effect. Most scientists claim that such treatments are no better than placebos.

A spokesman for the event said: 'We believe it is unethical for the government and Boots (as a registered pharmacist) to continue to support what is essentially an 18th century magic ritual.'

Paul Bennett, superintendent pharmacist for Boots UK, said that homeopathy was recognised by the NHS and that all Boots pharmacists followed guidance on homeopathy issued by the Royal Pharmaceutical Society of Great Britain.

Paula Ross, chief executive of the Society of Homeopaths, described the event as 'an ill-advised publicity stunt in very poor taste'.

The Guardian, 20 January 2010

Use of fact and opinion

Journalists tend to use both **fact** and **opinion** when writing articles. The extent to which they use facts and opinions often depends on their purpose. Is their aim to inform their reader? Are they trying to influence how the reader thinks about something?

Item 4.1 relies heavily on facts. The journalist is not seeking to influence the reader and therefore, generally, presents the facts as they stand. Opinions are included, but these are the opinions expressed by involved persons and it is a 'fact' that they have expressed them.

However, even when an article is written to inform, the selection of a fact and how it is presented can have an influence on the reader.

> **Key terms**
>
> **Fact:** something that can be proved to be true.
>
> **Opinion:** a point of view that cannot be proved to be true or untrue.

Activity

2   Look again at Item 4.1.

   a   Highlight the use of facts in this article.

   b   Highlight any opinions expressed in the article.

   c   Think about the fact: 'Most scientists claim that such treatments are no better than placebos.' What difference might it have made if the writer had given their views of the scientists who do not claim this?

   d   What comment(s) can you now make on the use of fact and opinion in this article?

Fact and opinion in argument

Often journalists construct an article around an argument, for example, that the school-leaving age should be raised to 18 or that 16-year-olds should be given the vote. They may draw on factual evidence to support their points or they may rely entirely on opinion. Their intention is almost always to influence the thoughts and feelings of their readers.

Activity

3   Read Item 4.2, an article on travel.

   a   As you read, jot down any facts which you come across.

   b   Write a couple of sentences which sum up the argument which the writer makes in this article.

Item 4.2

Mindless in Gaza

Jack Shamash

Here is a speck of comfort for anyone not planning to canoe up the Amazon or trek across Siberia – contrary to what anyone will tell you, travel does not broaden the mind.

It was the Victorians who were really obsessed with travel. They lived at a time when travel really did harden the body and improve the spirit. It took a rare breed of man to trudge through some malaria-infested swamp in a pith helmet, after the native bearers had drunk all the whisky, stolen the bully beef, and run off with the compass.

Since then, travellers have thought of themselves as faintly noble and they look down on mere tourists who stay in comfortable hotels and ride in air-conditioned buses. To travellers it is a mark of pride to suffer as much as possible. They get a perverse joy from spending all day squatting over a sordid cesspit.

Paul Theroux, a best-selling travel writer, is one of the people caught up in the myth: 'the nearest thing to writing a novel is travelling in a strange country.' Travel, he declares, is a creative act. It isn't. It may be interesting, but travellers get no insight into eternal truths.

Travellers learn a lot about shopping (good in Singapore, bad in China). They learn how to avoid the young boys that follow you everywhere in Morocco (look at them with a condescending smile). They discover how to find a pensione in Spain; what sort of Mexican food to avoid, or where to buy good hash in Tunisia. In doing so, they find out very little about Orientals, Arabs, Spaniards or Mexicans. A knowledge of Indian railway timetables and hotel prices is not the same as understanding Indian culture.

Travellers acquire useless skills such as how to make trivial conversation with new acquaintances – discussing cameras or makes of car is a sure-fire way of provoking long and boring discussions.

Many people use travel as an idiotic form of escapism. Oxford graduates, who would not be remotely interested in getting to know British working-class people on council estates, find it uplifting to go sightseeing among the poor of the Third World.

The worst travellers are the long-term ones – often people with personal problems who are keen, not so much to see the world, as to avoid returning home. As a rule, the only people who travel for more than a year are simpletons, social inadequates or New Zealanders.

Weekend Guardian, 12 October 1991

Did you notice that the only facts in the article occur when the writer refers to Paul Theroux as 'a best-selling travel writer' (which can be proved through reference to sales figures) and tells us that Theroux declares that 'travel is a creative act' (which can be proved through reference to his writing)?

For the most part the writer expresses opinions, though often these are stated as though they were facts, for example:

'… travel does not broaden the mind'

'Travellers learn a lot about shopping'

Activity

4 Look back through Item 4.2.

    a Make a note of five other examples where opinion is stated as fact.

    b Suggest two reasons which would explain why the writer has chosen to state opinions as though they were facts.

When journalists wish to influence the reader they might:

- select only facts that support their point of view
- present opinions as though they were facts.

You need to show your examiner that you are aware of this.

Examining other techniques

Use of fact and opinion and reference to the words of relevant people are just a few of the techniques that journalists might use when writing an article. Other frequently used devices include:

- the deliberate exaggeration of certain points – this is sometimes called **hyperbole**
- the use of **rhetorical devices** such as rhetorical questions, repetition and groups of three
- the use of language to influence the feelings of the reader – this is sometimes called **emotive language** or **loaded language**.

You need to show your examiner that you are aware of these methods and the reasons for their use.

> ### Key terms
>
> **Hyperbole:** the deliberate exaggeration of one or more points.
>
> **Rhetorical devices:** techniques used to influence the reader such as rhetorical questions, groups of three and repetition.
>
> **Emotive language/loaded language:** words selected to affect the feelings of the reader.

Activity

5 Look again at Item 4.2.

    a Identify the use of hyperbole in the second paragraph. Explain why you think the writer has used this.

    b Identify two groups of three. Choose one of them and explain why you think the writer has used this device in this place.

    c Identify two examples of words being selected to affect the feelings of the reader. For each example explain:

        i why you think those words have been chosen

        ii how the words are likely to affect the feelings of the reader.

Reading in the exam

When you are reading in the exam you need to be thinking hard – about meaning, language and tone. Here are some of the thoughts a student might have when reading the first half of Item 4.2.

Uses extreme examples – not most people's experiences

'Obsession' – generally a bad thing

Some sarcasm in tone

Attributes viewpoint to travellers without evidence

Unsupported assertion

Image of something disgusting

Refers to a well-known traveller

Suggests fantasy and make-believe

> Here is a speck of comfort for anyone not planning to canoe up the Amazon or trek across Siberia – contrary to what anyone will tell you, travel does not broaden the mind.
>
> It was the Victorians who were really obsessed with travel. They lived at a time when travel really did harden the body and improve the spirit. It took a rare breed of man to trudge through some malaria-infested swamp in a pith helmet, after the native bearers had drunk all the whisky, stolen the bully beef, and run off with the compass.
>
> Since then, travellers have thought of themselves as faintly noble and they look down on mere tourists who stay in comfortable hotels and ride in air-conditioned buses. To travellers it is a mark of pride to suffer as much as possible. They get a perverse joy from spending all day squatting over a sordid cesspit.
>
> Paul Theroux, a best-selling travel writer, is one of the people caught up in the myth: 'the nearest thing to writing a novel is travelling in a strange country.' Travel, he declares, is a creative act. It isn't. It may be interesting, but travellers get no insight into eternal truths.

Establishes argument in first paragraph and states opinion as fact

Opinion as fact

Uses hyperbole for added effect

Seems to be laughing at them

Suggests something wrong

Links with 'perverse' = bad

Simple statement of contradiction for effect

Sarcasm

Practice question

1 Imagine you are in the exam room. Reread the final four paragraphs of the article. Use the model above to help you annotate them with thoughts on meaning, language and tone.

Top Tip

Many students find it helpful to annotate or highlight texts in the exam.

Bias

By now you will have realised that Jack Shamash is strongly opposed to the idea that travel broadens the mind. He presents opinions as though they were facts and uses a range of techniques in order to influence the reader. In doing so he displays a strong **bias**. His argument is not balanced. It is biased.

When reading articles you need to be willing to question what the writer has said and to show your examiner that you are able to do this.

Here is a possible exam question:

> How are the thoughts and feelings of the writer revealed to the reader?

Key terms

Bias: a tendency towards a particular belief that can exclude other opinions.

To answer this well you need to show you have considered:

- what the thoughts and feelings are
- the techniques the writer uses to reveal them to the reader.

You need to show that you can examine a text closely, explore and infer meaning, and analyse language use.

Here is the first part of a student's response to the above question. The skills demonstrated by the student are annotated by an examiner for you. The following abbreviations have been used:

aw: awareness
struct: structure
tech: technique
ref: reference to textual detail
und: understanding

t.p.: technique and purpose
inf: inference
explo: exploration
anls: analysis

The writer's viewpoint is revealed in the opening paragraph ✓ when he states controversially and as though it were fact ✓ that 'travel does not broaden the mind' ✓. He then proceeds to develop this line of argument through a range of strongly stated opinions, ✓ regularly presented as facts, using emotive language to good effect.

  When referring to the Victorians, who lived in a time when according to the writer 'travel really did harden the body and improve the spirit' ✓ he still maintains an air of sarcasm ✓ in the reference to a 'rare breed of man' ✓ and the use of hyperbole to collate all the possible dangers which were faced. ✓ Perhaps, despite his words, he intends to suggest the Victorian traveller was not really worthy of admiration. ✓ His attitude to the modern traveller is, however, more severe. His reference to their 'perverse joy' ✓ suggests something inherently wrong and bad in what they do, ✓ almost as though they were criminals or misfits. ✓ The suggestion of something bad is sustained in the use of the word 'sordid' which has connotations of dirty and degraded. ✓ When combined with the image of ✓ 'spending all day squatting over a sordid cesspit' the reader is guided ✓ to feel repulsion and a touch of disgust ✓ for the modern day traveller.

Annotations (left): aw struct, aw tech, ref, aw struct, inf, ref, inf & explor, infer, und t.p.

Annotations (right): ref, und tech, explo, ref, inf, anls, anls

At the end of the full answer the examiner wrote this comment summarising the skills demonstrated by the student:

Examiner comment: The student explores meaning and makes valid inferences. There is analysis of language combined with a strong understanding of technique and purpose. These are all high-level reading skills.

2 Focusing on other aspects of how the thoughts and feelings of the writer are revealed to the reader, write a further paragraph. Aim to demonstrate high-level reading skills.

Use the model on page 29 to help you annotate your answer with examiner comments. Look for evidence of the ability to:

- examine a text closely
- explore and infer meaning
- analyse language use.

Check your revision

You are now going to find out whether you can make good use of the work you have done in this chapter.

Read Item 4.3, the article called Wild Thoughts, closely. While reading, highlight the text and make brief annotations on anything significant connected with meaning, language and tone.

Now answer the following questions.

Structure

- Summarise in one or two sentences the argument developed by Mark Carwardine in this article.
- At what point in the article are you first made aware of what the argument is?

Fact and opinion

1 Find examples of:
- facts used to develop the argument
- opinions used to develop the argument
- opinions stated as fact.

2 Why do you think Carwardine does not include facts to support his statement that 'ecotourism can be hugely beneficial'?

3 Writers will use emotive language even when presenting facts. Which word is used emotively in the following sentence and why do you think the writer has chosen to use it:

'One of its most shocking findings was a five-fold decline in the density of native carnivores in the areas where ecotourism was allowed.'

Examining other techniques

1 You need to demonstrate skills in analysis. This means that you can closely examine the use of language and develop comments on it. Read the following sentence and write a paragraph about the ways in which language is used for effect in it.

'Now, with visitor numbers increasing fast, it has become the latest in a string of wildlife hotspots that risk being loved to death by well-meaning ecotourists.'

2 The writer uses a group of three rhetorical questions in the final paragraph. Write an extended comment on:
- the questions and how they link with each other and the rest of the article
- significant features of language use
- the intended effect on the reader.

Bias and tone

1 Would you describe this argument as balanced or biased? Give reasons for your choice.

2 How would you describe the tone of this article? Give evidence to support your choice?

Item 4.3

MARK CARWARDINE
WILD THOUGHTS

I've just returned from photographing jaguars in the Pantanal, which happened to be the subject of Steve Winter's stunning portfolio in last month's *BBC Wildlife*. These big cats were notoriously difficult to see in the wild until quite recently, when word reached the outside world of a particular place where sightings are virtually guaranteed.

Now, with visitor numbers increasing fast, it has become the latest in a string of wildlife hotspots that risk being loved to death by well-meaning ecotourists.

Ecotourism can be hugely beneficial, of course, and there are cases where it has saved species from extinction. But just because it's labelled 'eco' doesn't necessarily make it OK.

A recent study by the University of California, for instance, compared a number of protected areas with and without ecotourism. One of its most shocking findings was a five-fold decline in the density of native carnivores in the areas where ecotourism was allowed.

One problem is sheer numbers. Fifty thousand people now visit Antarctica every year – five times as many as in the early 1990s. Nearly 180,000 people go to the Galápagos Islands; on my last visit to the islands, I saw a lone albatross on her nest surrounded by no fewer than three tour groups – 48 people in all.

Think pink: should river dolphins be protected from photographers?

But it is the sudden and unexpected growth in numbers that is causing special concern. A couple of years ago, *BBC Wildlife* published a portfolio of my Amazon river dolphin pictures. With hindsight, I should have anticipated the response – an onslaught from photographers wanting to know where to go. Within a year, what was once a quiet backwater became a media circus.

> On my last visit to the Galápagos, I saw a lone albatross on her nest surrounded by no fewer than three tour groups.

Should the Pantanal and the Amazon river dolphins have been kept secret for as long as possible? Should visitor numbers to Antarctica and the Galápagos be capped? These questions strike at the heart of one of the great conservation dilemmas of the day – how do we achieve a balance between encouraging (or merely allowing) people to watch and care for wildlife and protecting the very wildlife they come to see?

BBC Wildlife magazine, September 2009 (see also www.markcawardine.com)

More about comparison

To do well in your exam you need to be able to make effective comparisons between texts. Questions 1, 2 and 3 in your exam are each worth 8 marks. Question 4, the comparison question, is worth 16 marks. You have already considered some aspects of comparison in Chapter 3. In this chapter you are going to develop your skills further. To do this, you are going to look again at three Items. To make it easier, these Items have been renumbered as follows:

- Item 1 is the advert, Seattle: Gateway to your Washington State adventure (page 3)
- Item 2 is the review, True tribal style (page 10)
- Item 3 is the article, Mindless in Gaza (page 26).

Following instructions

You are asked to read and answer questions on three Items in your exam. Question 1 will be on Item 1, question 2 on Item 2 and question 3 on Item 3. Question 4 will name one Item and ask you to select another one with which to compare it. The instruction will look something like this:

> You must choose between the other two items

> Title of named item

> Named item which you **must** write about

Now you need to refer to Item 3, Mindless in Gaza, and **either** Item 1 **or** Item 2. You are going to compare two texts, one of which you have chosen.

It is important to read this instruction carefully. You would be surprised at how many students do not write about the named Item and end up losing marks unnecessarily. Notice that while the example above names Item 3, the named Item could be 1 or 2.

Make sure you go on to read the actual question before you make your choice of text as you need to choose the Item that is going to help you to write a good answer.

The instructions and the question will look like this:

> Now you need to refer to Item 3, Mindless in Gaza, and **either** Item 1 **or** Item 2. You are going to compare two texts, one of which you have chosen.
>
> **4** Compare the ways in which language is used for effect in the two texts. Give some examples and explain what the effects are.

Making a good choice

Now that you know that you have to focus on the use of language, you are in a position to choose your Item.

Remind yourself of Items 1, 2 and 3 (pages 3, 10 and 26) and the work you did on the use of language in each of these three texts in Chapters 1, 2 and 4.

Item 1

SEATTLE: GATEWAY TO YOUR WASHINGTON STATE ADVENTURE.

Seattle: the perfect mix of experiences. Cosmopolitan and casual. Industrious and playful. High-tech and hand-crafted. Urban and natural.

With over 25 international flights arriving regularly, Seattle is the perfect gateway to begin your exploration of Washington, and the Pacific Northwest.

Experience the city's renowned restaurants, shops and cultural attractions. Jump on a ferry to nearby islands. Take a day trip to the mountains or the rainforests, or journey east to the high desert and wine regions. It's all here.

Oh, and we also make a pretty good cup of coffee.

To begin your journey, please visit www.ExperienceWA.com

Or contact our local representative:

In the United Kingdom: First Public Relations Tel: +44 (20) 7978 5233 Fax: +44 (20) 7924 3134 web: www.firstpr.co.uk

In Belgium, Netherlands and Luxembourg: BuroSix Tel: +31 (0) 182 39 44 55 Fax: +31 (0) 654 28 03 32 info@burosix.nl www.burosix.nl

ExperienceWA.com
Washington State Tourism

Item 2

True tribal style

Venture into the mysterious world of Ethiopia's Surma and Mursi tribes with this striking book of portraits.

Dawn breaks in Ethiopia's isolated Omo Valley. For the tribespeople it's another typical day: collecting water, herding goats and ... getting dressed up.

Life here can be bleak; the arms and ivory trades flourish and guerrilla warfare is commonplace. But all this is punctuated by rather more innocent pursuits. Just for the fun of it, the Omo's men, women and kids indulge in a daily, centuries-old rhythm of fancy dress. And we're not talking a half-hearted effort either: when it comes to costumes, make-up and elaborate headgear, the Omo tribes really go to town.

Photographer Hans Silvester has journeyed to their homeland 12 times. His latest tome is bursting with dazzling portraits showcasing their penchant for body adornment. The shots reveal theatrical headdresses fashioned out of banana leaves, necklaces made of snail shells and naked limbs smeared with volcanic body paint.

Other more unsettling get-ups involve monkey skins, butterfly wings and lip disks – women create painful holes in their lower lip and insert round plates, thus increasing their chances of snagging a rich husband.

The book doesn't offer an intimate peek inside the tribes' daily lives. Indeed, some of the portraits look so exquisitely styled they smack of a *Vogue* photo shoot, leaving you wondering if it's all just a contrived show for the camera. But this is an intrinsic part of their culture, and would continue regardless of whether our eyes were on them.

'Body painting, as practised here in east Africa, the cradle of humanity, ... represents a way of life that dates from prehistory,' muses Silvester. 'Perhaps underlying it all is the spirit of the hunter, accustomed to camouflage ... or perhaps it is simply and unconsciously homage to Mother Earth.'

Whatever drives the Omo people to get kitted out in their finery, it's impossible not to marvel at the visual spectacle. You'll be entranced by this striking record of a fascinating but increasingly fragile community. **Anna Webber**

Natural Fashion, Hans Silvester (Thames & Hudson, £18.95)

Item 3

Mindless in Gaza

Jack Shamash

Here is a speck of comfort for anyone not planning to canoe up the Amazon or trek across Siberia – contrary to what anyone will tell you, travel does not broaden the mind.

It was the Victorians who were really obsessed with travel. They lived at a time when travel really did harden the body and improve the spirit. It took a rare breed of man to trudge through some malaria-infested swamp in a pith helmet, after the native bearers had drunk all the whisky, stolen the bully beef, and run off with the compass.

Since then, travellers have thought of themselves as faintly noble and they look down on mere tourists who stay in comfortable hotels and ride in air-conditioned buses. To travellers it is a mark of pride to suffer as much as possible. They get a perverse joy from spending all day squatting over a sordid cesspit.

Paul Theroux, a best-selling travel writer, is one of the people caught up in the myth: 'the nearest thing to writing a novel is travelling in a strange country.' Travel, he declares, is a creative act. It isn't. It may be interesting, but travellers get no insight into eternal truths.

Travellers learn a lot about shopping (good in Singapore, bad in China). They learn how to avoid the young boys that follow you everywhere in Morocco (look at them with a condescending smile). They discover how to find a pensione in Spain; what sort of Mexican food to avoid, or where to buy good hash in Tunisia. In doing so, they find out very little about Orientals, Arabs, Spaniards or Mexicans. A knowledge of Indian railway timetables and hotel prices is not the same as understanding Indian culture.

Travellers acquire useless skills such as how to make trivial conversation with new acquaintances – discussing cameras or makes of car is a sure-fire way of provoking long and boring discussions.

Many people use travel as an idiotic form of escapism. Oxford graduates, who would not be remotely interested in getting to know British working-class people on council estates, find it uplifting to go sightseeing among the poor of the Third World.

The worst travellers are the long-term ones – often people with personal problems who are keen, not so much to see the world, as to avoid returning home. As a rule, the only people who travel for more than a year are simpletons, social inadequates or New Zealanders.

If you were to answer the exam question on page 32, you would have to write about Item 3 (Mindless in Gaza) and make a choice between Item 1 (Seattle: Gateway to your Washington State adventure) and Item 2 (True tribal style). In order to make a good choice you need to ask yourself: Which Item will enable me to:

- make interesting comparisons with Item 3
- demonstrate high-level reading skills when writing about the use of language for effect?

Practice question

1 Make brief notes on the points you could make in an answer if you chose to compare Item 3 and Item 1.

Make brief notes on the points you could make in an answer if you chose to compare Item 3 and Item 2.

Decide which Item you would choose and list your reasons for doing so.

When answering the question on page 32, you could choose either Item 1 or Item 2. Both items provide plenty of material for you to write about. It is a case of choosing the one that you think you can make best use of. However, this is not always the case. Think about the following question:

> Now you need to refer to **Item 1**, Seattle: Gateway to your Washington State adventure, and **either** Item 2 **or** Item 3. You are going to compare two texts, one of which you have chosen.
>
> 4 Compare the ways in which presentational features are used for effect in the two texts. Give some examples and explain what the effects are.

Top Tip

Always think carefully about which Item to choose for the comparison question. Making a good choice will help you to gain good marks.

Item 3 would be a very poor choice for this question as it does not have many presentational features. You would be severely limiting what you could write if you chose this item.

Thinking about timing

You are advised at the start of your paper to spend an hour on Section A. In that time you need to:

- read three texts closely
- answer three questions worth 8 marks each
- answer one question worth 16 marks.

The exam paper advises you to read Item 1 and answer the question on it before moving on to read Item 2 and answer the question on it. By the time you reach Question 4, you have read all of the texts but you need to look at a new aspect of two of them.

As a rough guide, you need to spend about 14 minutes on each of Questions 1–3, which includes time for reading the Items. This leaves you about 18 minutes for Question 4.

Alternatively, you could spend 10 minutes reading Items 1, 2 and 3 and the questions. This then allows 10 minutes to answer each of Questions 1–3 and 20 minutes to answer and check Question 4.

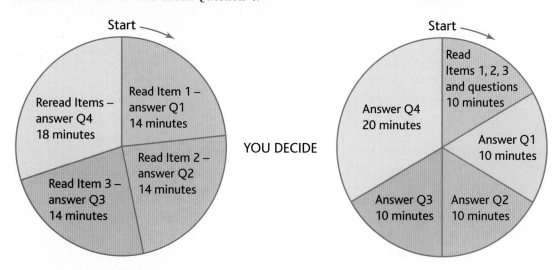

It is important that you keep a close eye on the clock during your exam. You cannot afford to spend more than an hour on Section A. Section B also needs your time.

Starting your answer

Don't waste time writing an 'introductory' paragraph telling the examiner what you intend to do. Aim to focus immediately on what the question has asked you to do.

Activity

1 Compare the following opening paragraphs that answer the question on page 32.

page 32

Student A

> I am going to compare Item 1, Seattle: Gateway to your Washington State adventure, with Item 3, Mindless in Gaza. Item 1 is an advertisement for Seattle and Item 3 is a piece of travel writing in which the writer argues that travel is not a good thing. These Items use language in different ways to influence the reader and make him or her think. I am going to write about some of the similarities and differences between them and comment on their effect.

Student B

> These Items have different intended purposes and the use of language in them reflects this. Item 1 is an advertisement designed to persuade the reader to visit Seattle. The writer repeatedly addresses the reader directly, the first time being in the title where he uses the pronoun 'your'. The writer of Item 3 also addresses the reader directly early on using the pronoun 'you' (contrary to what anyone will tell you) but not after this. Instead, his focus is on the development of his argument.

Top Tip

Answer the question right from the start, using textual detail to support the points you make.

- Which one refers to a specific technique?
- Which one uses textual detail to support the reference?
- Which one compares how a technique is used in both texts?
- Which one will gain the most marks?

Thinking about the mark scheme

Examiners use a mark scheme to help them assess your work. The mark scheme is divided into bands. Bands 3 and 4 define the skills of students likely to get a Grade C or above. In the table on page 36 you will see what is expected of students in these bands when answering this question:

4 Compare the ways in which language is used for effect in the two texts. Give some examples and explain what the effects are.

The higher-level qualities of Band 4 are highlighted for you.

Band 3	Band 4
Clear evidence that the texts are understood	Offers a full and detailed understanding and interpretation of content of the texts
Shows clear appreciation and analysis of words and phrases in different contexts	Shows a detailed and perceptive appreciation, interpretation and analysis of how the writers have used language differently to achieve their effects and to attain impact
Offers relevant and appropriate quotations and references to support ideas	Offers full relevant quotation in support of ideas with appropriate and perceptive comments
Present tense, clear focus on comparisons and cross-references between the two texts	Focuses on comparison and cross-referencing between the texts and throughout the response

These are the skills examiners will be looking for. Most examiners are teachers. They want students to do well. They want to give you good marks. But, they cannot give you the marks unless you demonstrate the skills.

Top Tip

To match the requirements of Band 4, you need to show that you can analyse language in detail and perceptively interpret the different ways in which language is used.

Practice question

2 Read the following comments made by students as part of a response to the question:

> **4** Compare the ways in which language is used for effect in the two texts. Give some examples and explain what the effects are.

The comments are based on Item 3 and Item 1. They show understanding, offer relevant quotation and there is a clear focus on comparison so they would be placed in Band 3. Use the prompts to help you develop each comment to move it to the top of Band 3 and up into Band 4.

Comment 1

> *The writer of Item 1 chooses words to make Seattle sound attractive, such as 'Cosmopolitan and casual', whereas the writer of Item 3 focuses on unpleasant things about travel such as 'squatting over a sordid cesspit'.*

- Examine the contrast in 'cosmopolitan and casual'; comment on what is suggested by it.
- Analyse the connotations of 'squatting', 'sordid' and 'cesspit'; comment on the effect of using them together.

Comment 2

> *The writer of Item 1 uses words such as 'adventure' and 'exploration' to make the readers feel that they will have lots of new experiences. This is different to the technique used by Jack Shamash where he makes it all sound quite boring: 'Travellers learn about shopping'.*

- Examine the implications of the words.
- Think about and comment on the contexts of the words.
- Consider the effects of the words on the reader.

Structuring your answer

A common mistake made by students is that they try to write about everything and end up making relatively simple comments. You do not have time to cover everything. What you *do* need to do is show that you have high-level reading skills. To do this you need to make good choices when selecting what to focus on.

In the previous practice question, you considered comments about Item 3 and Item 1. You are now going to think about comparing the ways in which language is used for effect in Item 2 and Item 3.

Start by identifying a feature of language that is found in both items, such as the use of emotive or loaded language to influence the feelings or attitude of the reader.

Then list examples from both texts:

> ### Item 2 (True Tribal Style)
> Life here can be bleak
>
> a daily, centuries-old rhythm
>
> impossible not to marvel at
>
> increasingly fragile community

> ### Item 3 (Mindless in Gaza)
> a mark of pride to suffer
>
> a perverse joy
>
> caught up in the myth
>
> an idiotic form of escapism

A quick look at the examples shows that Silvester uses language to make the reader think of the Omo people in a positive way, whereas Shamash uses words to make the reader see the modern traveller in a negative way.

Once you have got to this stage you are ready to write your comment. In your answer you should aim to write two or three developed paragraphs.

Practice question

3 Write a paragraph about the ways writers use language to influence their readers in Item 2 and Item 3. Remember to:

- analyse the uses of language
- make perceptive comments
- explore meaning and implications
- refer to the text to support the points you make
- point out similarities and differences between the writers' uses of language.

Many students think they have to write some kind of conclusion summing up all of the points they have made. You do not need to do this. It wastes time and gains you no extra marks. Try to end, as you started, with a comment that displays high-level reading skills. Remember, you want your examiner to be ticking your answer right up to the final sentence.

Check your revision

You are now going to find out how well you have understood the work in this chapter. We will use three of the Items that you saw in earlier chapters. Again, these have been renumbered as follows:

- Item 1 is the advert, Washington State: green before green was cool (page 9)
- Item 2 is the review, Tony Hawk Ride (page 17)
- Item 3 is the article, Wild Thoughts (page 31).

Making a good choice

Read the following question and highlight key words in it.

> Now you need to refer to Item 3, Wild Thoughts, and **either** Item 1 **or** Item 2. You are going to compare two texts, one of which you have chosen.
>
> **4**   Compare the ways in which language is used for effect in the two texts. Give some examples and explain what the effects are.

Remind yourself of these Items and the work you did on the use of language in each of the three texts.

Decide which text you would choose to write about if you were answering this question. List the reasons for your choice. Your reasons should be linked with the question and the high-level skills you are required to demonstrate.

Starting your answer

Write an opening paragraph for an answer to this question. Remember to:

- refer to a specific technique
- use textual detail to support the reference
- compare how the technique is used in both texts.

Thinking about the mark scheme

Write a paragraph on the way language is used to influence the feelings or attitudes of the reader in Item 3 and the Item you have selected. Remember to:

- analyse the uses of language
- make perceptive comments
- explore meaning and implications
- refer to the text to support the points that you make
- point out similarities and differences between the writers' uses of language.

Item 1

HOH RAINFOREST, OLYMPIC NATIONAL PARK

WASHINGTON STATE:
GREEN BEFORE GREEN WAS COOL.

Less than 100 miles from the urban metropolis of Seattle lies a mystical world. Lush, green, quiet, moss-covered, fresh-scented, the Hoh Rain Forest is a "must see" for any world traveler. The Hoh and the Quinault Rain Forests, both located in Washington's Olympic National Park, are just two of the reasons that the Olympic National Park has been named a UNESCO World Heritage Site and an International Biosphere Reserve.

Here you can walk, hike, bike, raft or kayak through primeval forests, experience mineral-rich hot springs, or enjoy 70 miles of rugged coastline.

The Olympic National Park...just one of the boundless discoveries you will find in Washington, the state.

To begin your journey, please visit www.ExperienceWA.com

Or contact our local representatives:

In the United Kingdom:	In Belgium, Netherlands and Luxembourg:
First Public Relations	BuroSix
Tel: +44 (20) 7978 5233	Tel: +31 (0) 182 39 44 55
Fax: +44 (20) 7924 3134	Fax: +31 (0) 654 28 03 32
web: www.firstpr.co.uk	info@burosix.nl
	www.burosix.nl

ExperienceWA.com
Washington State Tourism

Item 2

Add Game | Tag | Print | Email | Facebook | Digg | Tweet

Tony Hawk Ride
- Activision
- Robomodo
- Skateboarding
- Release: Dec 4, 2009
- PEGI

Also on: More info
X360 WII

Summary

Reviews
GameSpot Review ›
Player Reviews
Critic Scores

News
Previews & Features
Images
Videos
Answers
Hints & Cheats
Forum

Games you may like...

TONY HAWK'S

Hawk's Proving Ground (PS3)

TONY HAWK'S

Tony Hawk's Project 8 (PS3)

skate

Skate (PS3)

skate 2

Skate 2 (PS3)

Tony Hawk Ride Review

Busted controls and stripped-down gameplay make Tony Hawk Ride an overpriced fiasco.

The Good
The included skateboard peripheral is durable.

The Bad
Movements don't register correctly much of the time ● Bad menu organization and other presentation issues ● Challenge mode stinks, and every mode is stripped ● Tiny skating areas ● Really expensive.

Tony Hawk Ride is the ultimate triumph of gimmick over game. The concept: build a skateboard peripheral that lets players simulate skateboarding in their living rooms. The result: half-functioning hardware that fails to function with consistency and a shallow game devoid of excitement. Vert skating and free skating are the only sources of mild enjoyment here, but the fun is too short lived to justify the whopping $120 price tag.

It's impossible to separate the board from the game. After all, Tony Hawk Ride must be played with the included skateboard peripheral. It takes some time to get used to the feel of the board, though your skating career begins with a number of tutorials that help you get on your feet, so to speak. From there, it's a matter of completing races, performing tricks for points, and nailing short challenges as you trudge your way through Ride's single-player experience. Fortunately, the peripheral is easy to set up and physically solid. It also feels weighty and resilient, as if ready to withstand hours of punishment.

Yet while the hardware can take a beating, the oft-useless board all too often fails to read your movements with the precision necessary for the game to deliver any amount of fun. Manuals, ollies, and nollies are relatively simple to pull off. You perform manuals much as you'd expect: by raising the nose or tail of the board in the air and holding the position. You do ollies by popping the nose into the air, while nollies, of course, are executed by popping up the tail. But, when Tony Hawk Ride starts expecting you to pull off anything more precise, it collapses.

Tricks that involve the infrared sensors on the front, back, and sides of the peripheral are arbitrary, working only some of the time. You swipe or hover your hand over these sensors when you want to perform finger flips and grabs. But these moves aren't consistent. If you fail the trick, you're never sure whether you swiped your hand across the sensor too early, held it there too long, or your movement wasn't recognized at all.

Tony Hawk Ride's flaws don't end with the lousy controls. The game feels half finished, offering up the most bare-bones experience possible. Don't expect skater-specific specials or large, high-concept levels. You can free skate, but most of the areas are small and none of them offer the fast-paced freewheeling of previous Tony Hawk games. This is partially because Ride seems to fancy itself a simulation, though it's hard to take it seriously as a sim when you inadvertently skate across the ceiling or happen upon pedestrians that exclaim their surprise when you almost run into them...in the middle of a skate park.

You see Tony Hawk Ride's shallowness everywhere. You see it in its bare-bones online modes, which very few people are playing. You see it in the visuals, which get the job done without a lick of energy or personality. And you see it every time you have to endure the rest of the challenge, even if you're bound to replay it because you failed the first trick. Tony Hawk Ride is a waste of money.

By Kevin VanOrd, GameSpot Posted Dec 4, 2009 12:12 am GMT

GameSpot Score
3.5
bad

Critic Score 22 reviews **4.9**
User Score 110 Voters **4.3**
Your Score Sign to rate **N/A**

About the rating system » | Review the Game

Game Emblems

The Bad

the-dude12
Tony Hawk Ride is a good fun game for the whole family.
Continue »
8.0 great

Jack_n_Coke07
Awesome idea, really odd execution....but still keeps you playing
Continue »
6.5 fair

Critic Scores	See All
PSX Extreme	4 / 10
IGN	5 / 10
VideoGamer	4 / 10
1UP	D+
Gamervision	5.5 / 10
GameZone	9.2 / 10
NZGamer	4.5 / 10
GamingExcellence	4 / 10

*The links above will take you to other Web sites and are provided for your reference. GameSpot does not produce or endorse the content on these sites.

Item 3

MARK CARWARDINE
WILD THOUGHTS

I've just returned from photographing jaguars in the Pantanal, which happened to be the subject of Steve Winter's stunning portfolio in last month's *BBC Wildlife*. These big cats were notoriously difficult to see in the wild until quite recently, when word reached the outside world of a particular place where sightings are virtually guaranteed.

Now, with visitor numbers increasing fast, it has become the latest in a string of wildlife hotspots that risk being loved to death by well-meaning ecotourists.

Ecotourism can be hugely beneficial, of course, and there are cases where it has saved species from extinction. But just because it's labelled 'eco' doesn't necessarily make it OK.

A recent study by the University of California, for instance, compared a number of protected areas with and without ecotourism. One of its most shocking findings was a five-fold decline in the density of native carnivores in the areas where ecotourism was allowed.

One problem is sheer numbers. Fifty thousand people now visit Antarctica every year – five times as many as in the early 1990s. Nearly 180,000 people go to the Galápagos Islands; on my last visit to the islands, I saw a lone albatross on her nest surrounded by no fewer than three tour groups – 48 people in all.

But it is the sudden and unexpected growth in numbers that is causing special concern. A couple of years ago, *BBC Wildlife* published a portfolio of my Amazon river dolphin pictures. With hindsight, I should have anticipated the response – an onslaught from photographers wanting to know where to go. Within a year, what was once a quiet backwater became a media circus.

Should the Pantanal and the Amazon river dolphins have been kept secret for as long as possible? Should visitor numbers to Antarctica and the Galápagos be capped? These questions strike at the heart of one of the great conservation dilemmas of the day – how do we achieve a balance between encouraging (or merely allowing) people to watch and care for wildlife and protecting the very wildlife they come to see?

Think pink: should river dolphins be protected from photographers?

> On my last visit to the Galápagos, I saw a lone albatross on her nest surrounded by no fewer than three tour groups.

6

Objectives

In this chapter you will revise:

how to get as many marks as you can in the exam.

Making your reading skills count in the exam

The essentials

- You are tested on your reading skills in Section A of your GCSE English or GCSE English Language paper. This is worth 20% of your final marks.
- You are advised to spend one hour on Section A.
- You will be asked to read three non-fiction Items and answer four questions. There will be one question on each Item, numbered 1 to 3.
- The fourth question will name one Item and ask you to choose a second Item and compare a specific feature, such as use of language, in the two Items.
- Questions 1, 2 and 3 in your exam are each worth 8 marks. Question 4, the comparison question, is worth 16 marks.
- All questions will be based on the Assessment Objectives (see page 1).
- Keep a close eye on the clock. You cannot afford to spend more than an hour on Section A – and you must answer all four questions.

Here are four examination questions. The marks awarded for each answer are given. The highlighted boxes would not appear on an exam paper. They explain what each question is asking you to do.

In the exam, you will write your answer on the actual paper and space is allowed for this. Do not feel that you have to fill the space. Remember it is the skills you demonstrate that gain you marks, not the amount you write.

Here you are being asked to:
- read and understand a text
- select material appropriate to purpose.

1 Read **Item 1**, the online flyer for the Shakespeare Schools Festival.

In your own words, explain the different things you learn about the Shakespeare Schools Festival from reading this online flyer?

(8 marks)

Here you are being asked to:
- explain and evaluate how writers use structural and presentational features to achieve effects and engage and influence the reader
- support your comments with detailed textual references.

2 Now read **Item 2**, an extract from Shakespeare's Houses and Gardens leaflet.

How are structural and presentational features used for effect in this text?

(8 marks)

Here you are being asked to:
- read and understand a text
- select material appropriate to purpose.

3 Now read **Item 3**, To do or not to do, an article taken from a teachers' magazine.

What are some of the thoughts and feelings the writer has about the ways students were taught in the school he visited?

(8 marks)

Here you are being asked to:
- collate from different sources and make comparisons and cross-references as appropriate
- explain and evaluate how writers use linguistic and grammatical features to achieve effects and engage and influence the reader
- support your comments with detailed textual references.

4 Now you need to refer to Item 3 and **either** Item 1 **or** Item 2.

Compare the ways in which language is used for effect in the two texts. Give some examples and explain what the effects are.

(16 marks)

Activity

1 The three texts referred to in this sample paper are printed on the next few pages. Read them closely. Make notes on the answers you would give to each question.

Item 1

Shakespeare Schools Festival

2010 Festival   About Us   Events   Support Us

Giving 11-18 year olds the chance to perform Shakespeare plays in professional theatres

"The best day of my life"

Keisha, Year 9

2010 Festival   *October - November 2010*   *more*

Since 2000 the Shakespeare Schools Festival (SSF) charity has been using the genius of Shakespeare to change the lives of young people. It is the largest youth drama festival in the UK and, to date, has put 75,000 young people on the stage. Teacher Workshops are provided by partners, the National Theatre, and Cast Workshops by partners, the National Youth Theatre of Great Britain.

SSF Partners

Telereal Trillium   The Transformation Trust   SEMPERIAN   National Theatre   national youth theatre

➡ **2010 Tshirts On Sale Now**
The commemorative 10th Anniversary Festival Tshirt is now on sale, don't miss out!

➡ **2010 Festival**
More information about the 2010 Festival, including the theatres involved, can be found here

➡ **Scripts & Resources**
Download everything you need for your production in our Resources section. Including notes from the NT Directors workshop.

About Us   *more*

Watch ARK schools performing as part of SSF

0:00 / 3:18

Events   *more*

Fundraising Gala Dinner
13 Jul 2009
The Shakespeare Schools Festival returned to the Middle Temple Hall.

Shake-up at Bosworth
12 Jun 2009
Shakespeare's *Richard III* was given a 21st century spin

Support Us   *more*

Support the Shakespeare Schools Festival (SSF) and enable more young people to access the arts through live, professional theatre.

As a registered charity, SSF relies heavily on the goodwill of private donors to continue its work with young people.

Please support us here!

Shakespeare Schools Festival
2nd Floor - Downstream Building
1 London Bridge
London, SE1 9BG
Tel: 0207 785 6497
Fax: 0207 785 6490
Email: enquiries@ssf.uk.com

Registered charity number: 1087596 | VAT Number: 771 7563 04 | Website design & build by Wil Grace on Drupal

www.ssf.uk.com

The Birthplace: So much to see, learn, and experience

NEW FOR 2009

LIFE, LOVE & LEGACY
EXHIBITION

A FASCINATING
AND IMMERSIVE JOURNEY

A NEW INTRODUCTION TO
WILLIAM SHAKESPEARE

Visit our unmissable new exhibition at Shakespeare's Birthplace. It tells the wonderful story of the dramatist.

This enthralling experience interweaves theatre with Shakespearian magic and you will see real treasures and artefacts, associated with the man himself, including Shakespeare's First Folio, brought to life!

SHAKESPEARE ALOUD!

LIVE
PERFORMANCES AT
THE BIRTHPLACE

MEET YOUR FAVOURITE SHAKESPEARE CHARACTERS

Step into the Bard's imagination and see and hear his most intriguing characters come alive. You could catch Lady Macbeth sleepwalking through the corridors, witness the romantic meeting of Romeo and Juliet in the garden or see the ghost of Hamlet's father appear before your very eyes!

Daily from April to October

Shakespeare | FOUND
a life portrait

EXHIBITION
AT THE BIRTHPLACE
FROM 23 APRIL

This ground-breaking exhibition presents compelling evidence that this is the first and only portrait of Shakespeare painted in his lifetime.

Be among the first to share this defining moment in our understanding of Shakespeare. Fresh, startling, and daring, this is an opportunity to get as close as anyone has ever been to knowing what Shakespeare looked like. Find out for yourself how handsome and alive Shakespeare now seems after 400 years.

'BEHOLD AND WONDER'

ONLY UNTIL 6 SEPTEMBER

BOOK ONLINE & SAVE 10%: www.shakespeare.org.uk

All tickets are valid for 12 months so you can come back for free

Item 3

To do or not to do

I was invited for interview at a local school which, from a distance, I had always admired. It sparkled in the league tables whilst the comprehensive, my home for the last eight years, regularly skulks in a worthy but not glittering mid-way position. It's not that we don't try hard. We do. And so do our students. But there are reasons for the differences in achievement, perhaps most notably that for 40% of our students English is not their first language. The fact that they are 100% fluent in at least one other language has little impact on league tables, and no allowance is made for the difficulties of studying a subject such as science in a language which is not your own. All that aside, I looked forward to my visit. I was keen to observe, to learn and, perhaps, to get a senior teaching post.

The day started with a walk around the school. As my journey progressed, so my concerns grew. In classroom after classroom students sat in rows, the teacher stood at the front and all eyes (apart from those of the inevitable but rare miscreant) were on the whiteboard. Now, let me state at the outset that I am a great fan of the interactive whiteboard. It allows me, at the touch of a key, to visually enhance my teaching, to recall yesterday's lesson and to provide additional appropriate stimulus for those who require it. But, and it is a big but, it is only a tool, a glorified blackboard, as good (and no better) than its user. It is variety that keeps students engaged and stimulated and yet, as I walked through the silent corridors, I saw no evidence of students working in groups, no evidence of discussion, no evidence of active learning and, most significantly, no evidence of Drama.

Why has the research of the past been thrown away so readily for a mere machine? Have we simply forgotten how Drama builds confidence in students, helps them to question and challenge, stimulates the growth of their imagination and develops a plethora of other skills. Drama gets students and teachers alike out from behind the security of their desks and throws them into a world where the outcome is uncertain and yet to be discovered. The teacher is no longer the 'deliverer' of a tightly bound package neatly sellotaped to meet a list of dry objectives, but the facilitator of learning, the true educator.

A screen, no matter how 'interactive' bears no comparison with actual activity – just as the watching of a sport does not replicate the participation in it. As a teaching tool, Drama stimulates and concentrates the thinking processes. Why is the extensive research, documented over several decades in the last century by national experts such as Dorothy Heathcote, now in her eighties and still working, being ignored in favour of the passive approach? Is it fear of losing control that leads to a belief that students must be restrained in rows and forced face forward? Or maybe it's concern about what the OFSTED Inspector will think, or the parent bullied into a belief that the only good child is a placid one. Whatever the reasons, I knew it was not for me nor for the students I hope to have the privilege of teaching in years to come. At lunchtime, I gave my reasons and left. I had learnt a useful lesson. It is not just diamonds that sparkle; shards of broken glass do too.

The answers

You have one hour in which to read three texts and answer four questions. You need to give focused answers. The following activities will help you to do this.

2 Remind yourself of Question 1 (page 40).

Below are two students' answers to this question and the examiner's comments on them.
Read both answers and list the qualities that make the second answer better than the first.

First student

The flyer makes it clear that the festival takes place in October to November 2010 and has been running since 2000. We are given a list of facts about the festival in the first paragraph which says that it is the largest youth festival and that it has put 75,000 young people on the stage and that it runs Teacher Workshops and Cast Workshops. It is a registered charity and it runs fundraising events such as the Gala Dinner presumably to raise money to pay for the festival. You can highlight this to find out more about it. It has five different partners: Telereal Trillium, The Transformation Trust, Semperian, National Theatre and National Youth Theatre.

Examiner comment: This student was awarded 5 marks. The student selected a wide range of literal detail in the text appropriately and put this in their own words. They also made some connections between different details and showed awareness of the text's function as an online flyer and the opportunities this offers for revealing more information.

Second student

From reading the flyer we quickly learn a range of facts about the festival. For example, that it has been running since 2000, is the largest youth festival, has put 75,000 children on the stage, is a registered charity and has five distinct partners, demonstrating its significance as a national event. Less obvious details, however, are revealed through the images. We see a large group of students participating on stage. It looks interesting and active and shows that this is open to boys and girls of all ethnic backgrounds. The expressions of the students on the webcam also suggest that this is an experience not to be missed. Red is a dramatic colour and its use seems to emphasise not only what the SSF does but also the exciting nature of its work. As well as learning these things from what is immediately revealed to us, we are shown other things that could be learnt at the click of a mouse. By following the appropriate links we could find out how to audition, support the SSF as a private donor or register now, a link which is given particular emphasis through the vibrant use of red on black.

Examiner comment: This student was awarded 8 marks. The student effectively selected key facts and based inferences on these. Additionally, they explored the significance of the images, making perceptive comments on their implications, and clearly understood and appreciated the text's function as an online flyer.

Activity

3 Remind yourself of Question 2 (page 40).

The following student was awarded 5 marks.
The highlighted text shows you the skills that were demonstrated.

a Read the response and the annotations:

Green describes what is seen.

Blue begins to analyse the image.

Yellow links the feature to the written content of the text.

Pink explains; it starts to explore and evaluate effect.

> The text is divided into 3 columns connected by the border at
> the top and the bottom. Each column deals with something
> different and has its own individual heading, pictures and
> written text. This makes it easy to see at a glance the different
> things you can do or see there. Each column is also set apart
> by the colour which is used. The lighter colour blue is used in
> the central column which shows Shakespeare's house in the
> daytime. This makes you realise there are things to do outside
> the house as well as inside. The colour red is used dramatically
> to highlight specific points with the splodge in the print of
> 'aloud' making it look like Shakespeare has written it with an
> old pen. The word 'aloud' however also draws attention to what
> we learn from the print about how characters can be heard.
> The picture itself also shows an actor or guide in a part. In the
> first column we see young children looking at a book whereas
> the people in the second column look like teenagers. This shows
> that this place has things to interest people of different ages.
> It shows that there is a lot to see, learn and experience there
> which is what it tells you in the heading.

In order to gain higher marks the student would need to show she could:

- analyse the images individually and collectively in more detail
- make more perceptive comments when linking images to written content
- develop exploration and evaluation of effect.

b List additional points this student could have made that would demonstrate these high-level reading skills.

4 Remind yourself of Question 3 (page 40). Here you are being asked to:

- read and understand a text
- select material appropriate to purpose.

In order to answer this question well you need to identify and interpret thoughts and feelings. Look at the two examples below.

Example 1

> The writer had always admired the school where he had the interview as it did better in the league tables than the school where he taught. He was looking forward to his visit there.

Example 2

> The writer was looking forward to his visit to the school which did so well in the league tables when compared with his own school. However, it is clear that he believes the league tables are unfair as they do not take into account the difficulties some students have to overcome, such as not having English as a first language, nor many of the skills they have, such as speaking a number of other languages fluently.

To do or not to do

I was invited for interview at a local school which, from a distance, I had always admired. It sparkled in the league tables whilst the comprehensive, my home for the last eight years, regularly skulks in a worthy but not glittering mid-way position. It's not that we don't try hard. We do. And so do our students. But there are reasons for the differences in achievement, perhaps most notably that for 40% of our students English is not their first language. The fact that they are 100% fluent in at least one other language has little impact on league tables, and no allowance is made for the difficulties of studying a subject such as science in a language which is not your own. All that aside, I looked forward to my visit. I was keen to observe, to learn and, perhaps, to get a senior teaching post.

The day started with a walk around the school. As my journey progressed, so my concerns grew. In classroom after classroom students sat in rows, the teacher stood at the front and all eyes (apart from those of the inevitable but rare miscreant) were on the whiteboard. Now, let me state at the outset that I am a great fan of the interactive whiteboard. It allows me, at the touch of a key, to visually enhance my teaching, to recall yesterday's lesson and to provide additional appropriate stimulus for those who require it. But, and it is a big but, it is only a tool, a glorified blackboard, as good (and no better) than its user. It is variety that keeps students engaged and stimulated and yet, as I walked through the silent corridors, I saw no evidence of students working in groups, no evidence of discussion, no evidence of active learning and, most significantly, no evidence of Drama.

Why has the research of the past been thrown away so readily for a mere machine? Have we simply forgotten how Drama builds confidence in students, helps them to question and challenge, stimulates the growth of their imagination and develops a plethora of other skills. Drama gets students and teachers alike out from behind the security of their desks and throws them into a world where the outcome is uncertain and yet to be discovered. The teacher is no longer the 'deliverer' of a tightly bound package neatly sellotaped to meet a list of dry objectives, but the facilitator of learning, the true educator.

A screen, no matter how 'interactive' bears no comparison with actual activity – just as the watching of a sport does not replicate the participation in it. As a teaching tool, Drama stimulates and concentrates the thinking processes. Why is the extensive research, documented over several decades in the last century by national experts such as Dorothy Heathcote, now in her eighties and still working, being ignored in favour of the passive approach? Is it fear of losing control that leads to a belief that students must be restrained in rows and forced face forward? Or maybe it's concern about what the OFSTED Inspector will think, or the parent bullied into a belief that the only good child is a placid one. Whatever the reasons, I knew it was not for me nor for the students I hope to have the privilege of teaching in years to come. At lunchtime, I gave my reasons and left. I had learnt a useful lesson. It is not just diamonds that sparkle; shards of broken glass do too.

In the second example the reader summarises effectively, explores meaning and interprets attitude.

5 Take each paragraph in turn. Aim to get an overview of the writer's thoughts and feelings and write one sentence that summarises these. Write a further two or three sentences that explore meaning and interpret attitude.

6 Reread the full passage. Write one or two sentences that summarise the change in the writer's view with regard to the school that he, at first, thought 'sparkled' in the league tables.

Activity

7 Remind yourself of Question 4 (page 40).

You **must** refer to Item 3 (To do or not to do) and you can **choose** either Item 1 or Item 2.

You are advised to choose **some** examples. It is much better to analyse two or three good examples from each text than to write about 10 examples in a superficial way.

Read the following paragraph from a student's answer and highlight where they have:

- made comparison and cross-referenced
- explained and evaluated how writers use language for effect
- supported their comments with detailed textual references.

> The writer of Item 3 is reflecting on a personal experience and the text is written in the first person. He constructs an argument with the clear intention of influencing his reader and persuading the reader to think as he does and the language used is clearly biased and 'loaded'. The whiteboard is both a 'glorified blackboard' and a 'mere machine'. Whilst in some ways the adjectives 'glorified' and 'mere' seem like opposites, here they are both used to belittle the whiteboard, with the alliteration in 'mere machine' making the description more memorable. The writer of Item 2 also uses words to influence and persuade the reader. However, he creates a positive rather than a negative impression through the use of adjectives such as 'unmissable', 'wonderful', 'intriguing' and 'compelling'. Together these adjectives entice the reader making them want to visit this place. Whilst these words create a sense of mystery, an idea of adventure is introduced with the triplet 'Fresh, startling, and daring'. This, the words suggest, is a place that offers something new and something different, further projecting the image of a place that must be visited.

8 Choose one other feature of use of language in Item 3 and a text of your choice. The feature of language does not have to be the same in both texts, though you will need to develop a valid point of similarity or difference. Write a paragraph in which you:

- examine the chosen feature in the first text
- make a point of comparison
- examine the chosen feature in the second text.

Now that you have worked through a sample paper and learnt how to show your high-level reading skills to the examiner, you are ready to tackle a practice paper on your own.

7

Practice examination for the reading section

The questions in the examination are based on the Assessment Objectives.

Here are four examination questions. The marks awarded for each answer are shown. To help you, additional notes are given explaining how the questions are linked to the Assessment Objectives.

Here you are being asked to:
- read and understand a text
- select material appropriate to purpose.

Read **Item 1**, the article called Famine in Ethiopia by Michael Buerke.

1   What do you learn about the writer's thoughts and feelings about the famine in Ethiopia from reading this article?

(8 marks)

Here you are being asked to:
- explain and evaluate how writers use structural and presentational features to achieve effects and engage and influence the reader
- support your comments with detailed textual references.

Now read **Item 2**, an extract from the Unicef charity appeal leaflet.

2   How do the layout and images add to the effectiveness of these pages from the leaflet?

(8 marks)

Now read **Item 3**, Gates gives billions for vaccine to save millions, which is a newspaper article. What do you learn about the writer's views of the exhibition at the British Museum from reading this article?

Here you are being asked to:
- read and understand a text
- select material appropriate to purpose.

3   What do you learn from Sarah Boseley's article about why and how the Gates Foundation is promoting vaccines for children in poor countries.

(8 marks)

Here you are being asked to:
- collate from different sources and make comparisons and cross-references as appropriate
- explain and evaluate how writers use linguistic and grammatical features to achieve effects and engage and influence the reader
- support your comments with detailed textual references.

Now you need to refer to Item 3 (Gates gives billions for vaccine to save millions) and **either** Item 1 **or** Item 2.

4   Compare the ways in which language is used for effect in the two texts. Give some examples and explain what the effects are. *(16 marks)*

Famine in Ethiopia

I'll never forget the day that I found out what desperate hunger is really like for so many millions of people, who live on the very borders of existence. My camera team and I had been filming the results of the Ethiopian famine. We had spent several days, watching people die in front of us, children as well as adults, and seen tens of thousands of poor Ethiopians who did not seem far away from that fate. We were, I realise now, in a mild state of shock. So much horror around; such an enormous scale of suffering.

It was a paradox of this famine that when we went into a village in the middle of the worst affected area we found a café of sorts that was not only open but sold Coca-Cola and bread rolls. We sat in the corner of this mud room and were about to have these things for breakfast when there was a commotion at the door.

There must have been several hundred starving people fighting for a chance to see somebody eating.

At the very front was an old man, lined and wiry. His eyes were wide and his hands were trembling. He fell to his knees and, very slowly, started to move towards us across the floor with both hands stretched out, begging, in front of him.

Who could have eaten under those circumstances? But what could we do? We gave the old man some bread and went out into the street and, in a pathetic sort of way, tried to break up the rolls to feed all those people.

I have never felt so useless and I'm sure my colleagues felt the same. There was really nothing any of us could say to each other for some time after.

Gates give billions for vaccine to save millions

By Sarah Boseley, Health Editor

Bill and Melinda Gates have announced one of the biggest charitable donations in history – an unprecedented $10bn (£6.24bn) investment in vaccines for children in poor countries over the next decade.

Speaking at the World Economic Forum in Davos, the Microsoft founder called for 'a decade of vaccines' to reduce child mortality dramatically by 2020. The money will save an estimated 8 million lives, the couple say. It will pay for a big push to step up coverage of existing vaccines, such as for diphtheria, tetanus and whooping cough, and new ones for pneumonia and diarrhoeal diseases, which are big killers of small children.

The Gates Foundation has made child immunisation the cornerstone of its work in the developing world. 'Vaccines are a miracle – with just a few doses, they can prevent deadly diseases for a lifetime,' said Melinda Gates. 'We've made vaccines our number one priority at the Gates Foundation because we've seen first hand their incredible impact on children's lives.'

The biggest charitable donation in history was from Warren Buffett, at the time the second wealthiest man in the world after Gates, and the Gates Foundation was the recipient. Buffett gave $30bn to help the foundation's work in the developing world.

Bill and Melinda Gates have already committed $4.5bn to the research, development and delivery of various vaccines. They have shown great interest in scientific and technological solutions to the problems of disease and development. The couple also fund work towards an Aids vaccine, which is still a long way off. Big progress has been made in other disease areas.

Last week the New England Journal of Medicine published the results of two studies, one in Mexico and the other in Africa, that showed a vaccine against rotavirus was effective not only at reducing cases of severe diarrhoea in under-fives but also cut deaths.

The foundation is also following a malaria vaccine that is in late stage trials in Africa. Results suggest it will be only 50–60% effective, but that could still save many thousands of lives on the continent.

The $10bn will go to the Global Alliance for Vaccines and Immunisation (Gavi), launched at Davos 10 years ago to find finance for vaccination programmes in developing countries. It has reached 257 million additional children with new and underused vaccine so far, which it estimates will prevent 5 million deaths.

GlaxoSmithKline, the British company researching the malaria vaccines, said it hoped Gavi would arrange a financing package once the trials were complete. Its chief executive, Andrew Witty, has pledged to take only a minimal profit, to be reinvested in malaria research.

The Guardian, 30 January 2010

Section B — Writing

Introduction

About the exam

Throughout your GCSE course you have been developing your skills in writing. These skills will help you to cope with the demands of the exam.

There is one exam paper in GCSE English and GCSE English Language. Its focus is: **understanding and producing non-fiction texts**.

Writing is tested in Section B of the paper.

You will be asked to complete two writing tasks: one shorter task worth 16 marks and one longer task worth 24 marks.

You have one hour in which to complete both writing tasks.

This section is worth 20% of your final marks.

The Assessment Objectives

To do well, you need to be clear on what skills you are being tested on. These are defined in the Assessment Objectives, which underpin the questions you will be asked in the exam, and the mark scheme that examiners use to assess your answers. The Assessment Objectives are printed below. The annotations show you what they mean in terms of the skills you need to show your examiner.

Aim to be clear, relevant and interesting

Show that you have a varied, adult vocabulary range

Communicate clearly, effectively and imaginatively, using and adapting forms and selecting vocabulary appropriate to task and purpose in ways which engage the reader.

Think about what you have been asked to write. Is it a letter? Is it an article? Is it the text for a speech or leaflet?

Always keep in mind what you have been asked to do

Always keep any named audience in mind – and the examiner!

Plan in advance so that your ideas are well organised

Organise information and ideas into structured and sequenced sentences, paragraphs and whole texts, using a variety of linguistic and structural features to support cohesion and overall coherence.

Use features such as rhetorical questions, repetition, similes, headings and sub-headings effectively and consistently

Make sure your writing is technically accurate

Use a range of sentence structures for clarity, purpose and effect, with accurate punctuation and spelling.

Use a mixture of simple, compound and complex sentences

Being prepared

When you take the exam you have one hour to complete the Writing section. This is not a lot of time in which to demonstrate all the skills you have accumulated in writing since starting your GCSE course. The following chapters will help you understand what is expected and ensure that you show the best of your writing skills in order to gain the most marks.

Answering the question

Many students do not do themselves justice in the examination. They make mistakes that could easily be avoided. Student A, whose answer is reproduced below, was answering the first task on the Writing paper. He had 25 minutes to answer the question.

Quiet
Exam in
progress

Activity

1 Read the question and the answer below before completing this table to assess what the student did well and what they did not do well.

Skill demonstrated	Level of achievement
The ideas are communicated clearly	some/most/all of the time
The appropriate form has been used	yes/no
The writing is appropriate to the purpose	yes/no
The writing is appropriate to the audience	yes/no
The writing is organised	quite well/well/very well
There is variety in the range of sentence structures	some/much
There is variety in the range of vocabulary	some/much
The spelling and punctuation are accurate	sometimes/usually/always

Write an article for a school or college website in which you inform students in your year about a recent school or college event.

Welcome to Nestlefield High, the school that aims to make sure that once you've arrived you'll want to stay. This is the most successful school in Birmingham and is one of the most popular. Anybody is welcome. If you come to this school we will guarantee to get you off to a great start in your life.

The school has a great atmosphere, the students are friendly and helpful and the teachers are amongst the best in the country. They take the time to listen to your problems and to really help you with your studies. Many of them are happy to stay behind in the evenings to give you extra help if you need it. It's not surprising that Nestlefield has outstanding exam results and that there is such a high demand for places.

The sporting facilities at Nestlefield are amazing. There are two football pitches, five tennis courts and a running track. There is also a brand new gym.

The ICT centre is also brand new and you can use the computers during dinner time as well as in your lessons.

If you like the sound of Nestlefield, then I recommend you apply for a place quick. This is because there is limited places and the school is at a high demand because of how successfull it is.

Hope to see you in September!

Activity

2 Compare your assessment with the examiner's. Did you identify similar features?

> **Examiner comment:** The writing is reasonably organised though some paragraphs lack appropriate development. Punctuation and spelling are generally accurate and there is some range in vocabulary and sentence structures. The main problem lies in the content, which is not appropriate to purpose (give information about a recent school or college event) or audience (students in your year).

As the examiner notes, the main problem is that the student has not written what they were asked to write. A few minutes spent reading the question and planning the content would have made a big difference.

Examiners frequently report that students often fail to answer the question and lose marks as a result.

> **Top Tip**
>
> Make sure you analyse the question and plan your answer.

Planning

Before writing, you need to analyse the question and plan your answer. Steps A to E show you what you need to do. In your exam you should spend 4–5 minutes on this, so you need to practise.

Step A

Analyse the question to work out your subject, purpose, audience and the form your writing needs to take. For example:

Form   Purpose

Write an article for a school or college website in which you inform other students about a recent school or college event.

Audience   Subject

This takes less than a minute, yet many students do not do even this.

Practice question

1 Analyse the following questions. For each one, work out its subject, purpose, audience and form.

- Write a letter to the Chair of Governors at your school or college in which you argue that the school day should be shortened.
- Write the text for a leaflet advising parents on the most effective ways of dealing with their teenage children.
- Write the text for a speech persuading students at your school or college to support the charity of your choice.

Step B

Jot down a range of ideas connected with the subject, for example:

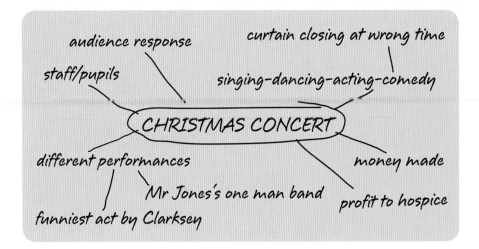

Practice question

2 Choose one of the writing tasks from Practice 1. Jot down a range of ideas connected with the subject.

Step C

Think about the order in which you are going to place your ideas. Aim to plan three or, at most, four coherent paragraphs. Remember, as this is the shorter writing task, you will only have about 20 minutes to write your response. You may think of new things as you do this, for example:

- Para. 1: rehearsals and range of acts – students and staff working together.
- Para. 2: Mr Jones's one-man band and Clarksey's performance.
- Para. 3: end of show – audience reaction – refer to money made (£520) and for good cause – link back to start, i.e. all the hard work worth it in the end!

Top Tip

Sometimes a very short, one-sentence paragraph can be effective, but take care not to overuse this device.

Practice question

3 Using your ideas from Step B, plan three or four coherent paragraphs. Remember you do not need to use all of your ideas and you can add new things that you think of.

Top Tip

When planning, select your best ideas to develop in more detail.

Step D

Remind yourself of the skills you need to demonstrate in your writing. You need to:

- engage and interest your student reader
- use standard English with a range of sentence structures and a varied, adult vocabulary
- make sure your writing is technically accurate.

Some students find it helpful to use a mnemonic to help them remember the main things they need to do. For example:

Standard English

Audience and purpose/accuracy

Varied vocabulary

Engage reader

Sentence structures

Practice question

4 Make up your own mnemonic, one that you could use in an examination, where each letter reminds you of what to do.

Step E

Think of an interesting opening that will engage your readers. Then start writing, for example:

> *The winter term can be the longest and dullest of them all. This year, things were different.*

Practice question

5 Think of the task you have chosen. Write three possible opening sentences that will engage your readers. Then choose the best one from these.

Top Tip

Linking your closing sentence to your opening one can be an effective structural device.

Developing your planning technique

> There is no doubt that proficient planning makes a significant difference to candidates' achievements.
>
> Principal Examiner's Report

Planning puts you in control of your writing. You know where you will start, where you will finish, which points you will develop in detail and how you will get from one point to the other.

Before you walk into your examination, you need to have developed an efficient way of planning that covers the five steps listed above and that works for you. Here are three examples of different students' plans for the question:

Sample question and answer

Write an article for a school or college website in which you inform other students about a recent school or college event.

Student A: list

purpose : inform
audience : students
form : article
subject : recent event

school show : Dec 8th

① lead up : preparation / rehearsals

② on the night – tension – behind the scenes – curtain raising

③ the best bits – C's solo – Mr J's magic act

④ applause – lights out – planning

Student B: spidergram

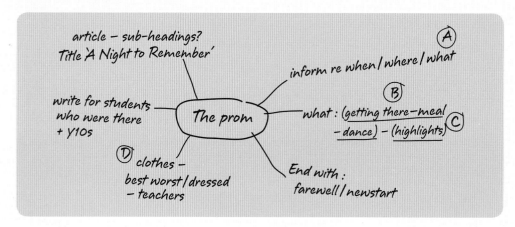

article – sub-headings?
Title 'A Night to Remember'

write for students who were there + y10s

The prom

Ⓐ inform re when / where / what

Ⓑ what : (getting there – meal – dance) – (highlights) Ⓒ

Ⓓ clothes – best worst / dressed – teachers

End with : farewell / newstart

Student C: ideastorm

Trip to France

Intro : Normandy – Easter – 25 y11s + 4 teachers – Hist + Lang

trip – Day 1 : Normandy landings : Day 2 : Bayeaux – Kate + Chris got 'lost' – meal in rest. Day 3 : graveyards – feelings / poetry reading

– Journey there + back – remember to give lots of info and make them

want to read on. Could do article in diary-type format?

Which of these plans is closest to the way you like to plan? Is there any way you could improve on it?

Activity

3 Choose another different writing task from the list shown in Practice 1. Spend five minutes planning your writing. Make sure you:

- gather a range of ideas
- decide on the order in which you will write about them
- remind yourself of the skills you need to demonstrate in your writing
- think of an engaging opening sentence.

Writing your answer

You are now almost ready to start writing your answer. There is one last thing you need to remind yourself of – TIME!

This is the short writing task which means that, after planning, you have about 20 minutes in which to write. To stay in control, you need to keep an eye on the clock. Your aim is to produce a complete piece of writing. It is better to leave a point out than to finish in the middle of nowhere. As soon as 15 minutes have passed, start thinking about how you are going to bring your writing to an end in the time you have left. Student A was successful in doing this. Make sure that you are.

Activity

4 Use the plan you made in Activity 3 as your guide, and spend 20 minutes writing your answer. Time yourself and keep your eye on the clock!

5 When you have finished writing, assess your writing honestly using the following assessment statements:

a I communicate my ideas clearly some/most/all of the time.

b My writing is/is not appropriate to purpose.

c My writing is/is not appropriate to audience.

d My ideas are sometimes/always organised in controlled paragraphs.

e My range of vocabulary is limited/varied/mature and sophisticated.

f My range of sentence structures is limited/varied/effective.

g My spelling and punctuation is sometimes/mostly/always accurate.

6 Using your assessment statements, set yourself one target for improvement.

 Top Tip

Aim to have a controlled ending to your writing.

Check your revision

Answer the following questions to make sure you have understood the work in this chapter:

- How long should you spend answering the first writing question?
- What do examiners say students often fail to do in their writing examination?
- Roughly how long should you spend planning an answer?
- What are the five stages of planning?
- What should you do after spending 15 minutes writing your answer to the first question?

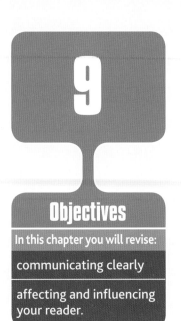

Key terms

Tone: the mood or atmosphere created through the choice of words.

Slang: words and phrases that are used in an informal context, often linked with certain regions or groups of people.

Standard English: the variety of English most used in public communication, particularly in writing.

Engaging your reader

On the front page of your exam paper you are reminded of the 'need for good English'. Remember, no matter whether you are writing for the Chair of Governors at your school or other students, you are always also writing for an examiner of English. Your ideas must be clearly expressed so that your meaning is communicated to your reader.

You can, however, vary the **tone** of your writing. If you are writing to your local MP, your tone is likely to be impersonal and formal. If you are writing to a friend, your tone is likely to be friendly and informal. However, you must avoid use of inappropriate **slang** or text language and, as a general rule, you should write in **Standard English**.

Activity

1 Read the following extracts from students' writing in the exam. They were all answering this question:

> Write a letter to a friend explaining why you would like him or her to join you in a visit to a place which you think is very special.

Identify where the students have:

● not communicated their ideas clearly

● not used Standard English.

Student 1

> After that, we could go shopping and buy loads and loads of exciting things to remind us of our stay at Blackpool or you could even win yourself some of the money you have spent in the arcades where there is a brill range of coin machines.

Student 2

> If u was to come with me to Bangladesh u will see a place that is very special. I would just love it if u could live with my big, noisy extended family for a while whom I have left behind and come here to Britain which I like very much as well.

Student 3

> We could visit Disneyland, Universal Studios, Big Bear town and Hollywood and having all these fab places around you will be awesome. The city of Los Angeles is great and is different to England where we go out shopping at 10am and finish at 5pm when everywhere is shut but people there and shops are open til about 11pm.

Did you notice that all three students use non-Standard English with words such as 'brill', 'u', 'fab', and 'til'?

Did you notice that none of the three students communicated their ideas clearly? For example: 'you could even win yourself some of the money you have spent in the arcades'; 'if you could live with my big, noisy extended family for a while whom I have left behind and come here to Britain'; 'but people there and shops are open til about 11pm.'

Practice question

1 Rewrite each of the three extracts in Activity 1 so that the ideas are communicated clearly and in Standard English.

Starting to write

Expressing ideas clearly in Standard English is only the start. You need to make your writing effective so that it will engage your reader from your opening sentence onwards.

About 50% of students start their writing using words from the task. For example, take the task:

> Write a letter to a friend explaining why you would like him or her to join you in a visit to a place which you think is very special.

One student might start like this:

> Dear Serena,
> There is a very special place which I would like you to visit with me ...

Another might start like this:

> Dear Matt,
> Last year I visited a really special place and I would very much like you to join me on a holiday there this year ...

And yet another might start like this:

> Dear TJ,
> I am going to explain why I would like you to join me on a visit to a place which I think is very special ...

Imagine being an examiner and reading all of these. Think how refreshing it is to find a student who does not open in a predictable way.

It is not difficult to do. There are several effective strategies that you can use. Here are three of them:

- A rhetorical question, for example:

> Dear Serena,
> Have you woken up recently to endless grey skies and wished you were somewhere more exciting?

- A series of short sentences, for example:

> Dear Matt,
> This is it. The chance of a lifetime is here. Read on.

- Description, for example:

> Dear friend,
> Before you read further, just imagine for a moment blue skies stretching endlessly above you and the warm sun shining on distant snow-capped mountain tops.

Top Tip

Avoid using key words from the question in your opening sentence.

Practice question

2 Using the techniques above, or others that you know of, write three engaging openings for each of the following tasks:

- A group of students from your school or college wants to go on an adventure trip abroad. Write the text of a speech to local business people persuading them to sponsor your group.

- Write an article for parents *advising* them on how to get their children to follow a healthier lifestyle.

For each task, decide which of your opening sentences is most likely to engage the reader.

How to keep your readers' interest

Once you have captured your readers' attention with an interesting opening, you need to keep it. To get a high grade, you need make sure that:

- the content of your writing is interesting and detailed
- you continue to show awareness of your reader.

It is sometimes easy to do one of these things but forget to do the other.

Activity

2 The following student is answering this task:

> Write an article for parents *advising* them on how to get their children to follow a healthier lifestyle.

The student starts well, by immediately addressing the reader and asking a rhetorical question. However, they then fall into the trap of relying too heavily on the same techniques.

Read the opening paragraphs of the student's writing and answer these questions:

a   How many rhetorical questions does the student ask?

b   How many times does the student use the word 'you' or 'your'?

c   How many exclamation marks does the student use?

> Do you as a parent want your children to be healthier, live life longer and grow up being fitter and stronger? If the answer to any of the above is yes, then keep reading! I'm going to advise you as parents on how to make the younger generation have a healthier lifestyle.
>
> Do you have a dog (or maybe another animal)? If you do … what are you waiting for? This is your opportunity. Get the kids up and you can all take the dog for a walk. If you have smaller or younger children, there are ways you can make it exciting for them. Why not play eye-spy or 'who can spot the … first'? For older children, why not invite a friend along?
>
> If you don't have an animal why not get your children involved in a club? Is there a sport your child really likes? It could be dancing, swimming, tennis or even skate-boarding! There are plenty of clubs around. They even have them at schools. So why don't you give sport a go? The whole family could join in. There is something for everyone out there!

The student above is writing at Grade C level. They write for their audience, communicate clearly and use some devices. However, they over-use the devices and there is little variety or range in the skills they are demonstrating to the examiner. This would prevent them from moving up to a grade higher than C.

> **Top Tip**
>
> Aim to show your examiner the full range of writing skills you have built up.

Practice question

3 Rewrite the second paragraph of the student's answer. Aim to describe a walk with children in a park or in the countryside and, through your description, make clear the benefits of this for the whole family. You may want to include details about:

- the different things you might see and hear
- the exercise you would get
- the opportunity it would provide for talking to your children.

Now rewrite the third paragraph. Focus on one or two sports that you know something about. Write about them and include interesting details and explain how they might benefit your readers' children.

How to manipulate your readers' response

Sophisticated writers do more than just engage their readers – they influence their ideas and their response in a variety of ways. Sometimes they do this through humour as in the following extract:

> I am a professional seagull spotter. Yes, you did read that correctly. It may sound silly but seagulls are seriously misunderstood birds. So, ask yourself, how much do you truthfully know about seagulls?
>
> Seagulls are beautiful, elegant birds. They are not pointless or useless, as some readers may think, but considerate and helpful. When the beach is buzzing and food is being dropped by the careless day-tripper, it is the kindly seagull who swoops in to clear up the mess. With unflinching nerve and not a whisper of complaint, the seagull acts as the unpaid rubbish collectors of our seaside towns. They deserve a medal and yet, their selfless actions are so often met not with an honorary distinction pinned to the chest, but with cries of dismay and the toe-end of a hobnailed boot.

Practice question

4 Write a paragraph of about 5–8 sentences in which you explain your interest in a particular sport, hobby or place. Aim to use humour in your writing to engage your reader. When you have finished, read through your writing and ask yourself if it would amuse your English teacher. If it would, then it will almost certainly amuse your examiner too.

Sometimes good writers use **anecdotes** to engage their readers, as in the following extract where the student is arguing for better care for the elderly.

> It was Mary who changed my mind. She was very frail and elderly, confined to a wheelchair and reliant on a machine to talk for her. She regularly dribbled on my lap as I helped her play bingo. We had just finished playing yet another game of bingo and I was simply sitting next to her, just watching the clock.
>
> Mary, using her sleeve, wiped the dribble from her chin and using her machine and finger began to type a message. I was poised ready for her to say that she needed the toilet. But, she didn't. After finishing her message, exhausted but smiling, she turned to me and played it aloud. In a bland and typical computer voice it announced, 'Ali is a nice young man.'
>
> I was emotionally devastated. This woman, who was so terribly disabled, had taken the trouble to comment that I was a nice young man, and all because I had spent some time with her. With those six words, my view of the elderly was changed forever.

Key terms

Anecdotes: short stories about particular people or events.

Top Tip

Using humour and anecdote can help you to influence your reader.

Practice question

5 Write a paragraph of about 5–8 sentences in which you use anecdotal information to support an argument for better facilities for young people in your area. Aim to use humour in your writing to engage your reader. When you have finished, write a sentence in which you explain how your anecdote supports your argument.

Other devices often used by good writers include repetition for effect, rhetorical questions, **emotive language/loaded language**, and presentation of **opinion** as though it were **fact**. The effective use of these devices is illustrated in the following extract where the student is aiming to persuade her reader to support a particular charity. The devices have been annotated for you.

Key terms

Emotive language/loaded language: words that are used to influence the way the reader feels about something or someone.

Opinion: a point of view that cannot be proved to be true or untrue.

Fact: something that can be proved to be true.

Top Tip

Rhetorical devices can be an effective tool. However, do not overuse them – be selective!

Emotive use of language – unacceptable, vulnerable, meagre morsel, plight

The situation is deteriorating at an unacceptable rate. By the end of this decade thousands more vulnerable children will be living without roofs over their heads, without fresh running water and without the means to buy even a meagre morsel of food. And still the developed world looks on. And still the developed world does nothing.

Repetition for effect – without and still the developed world

Opinion presented as fact

The fact is that while we can sympathise with the plight of a single child on our TV screens, it's too easy to become hardened to the spectacle of thousands of starving children waiting silently for our help. And yet, if we don't help, who will?

Rhetorical question

6 Write a paragraph of about 5 to 8 sentences in which you persuade your reader to support a charity of your choice. Aim to use some or all of the following devices:

- repetition for effect
- rhetorical question
- emotive use of language
- opinion presented as fact.

When you have finished, highlight and annotate your writing to show your use of devices to influence your reader.

Check your revision

Answer the following questions to make sure you have understood the work in this chapter:

- What form of English should you use in your writing in the exam?
- Name three techniques that you could use to engage your reader in the opening part of a piece of writing.
- What are the dangers of making too frequent use of the same devices?
- List four methods that you could use to influence your readers' ideas and response.

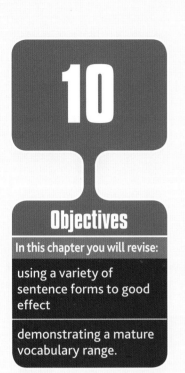

Sentence structures and vocabulary

Sentence structures

As you know, there are three main types of sentence.

Simple sentences

These are the first kind of sentences that you learn to write. A simple sentence consists of one main clause that makes complete sense on its own. Simple sentences always contain a subject and a verb, for example:

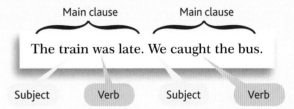

Compound sentences

These have two or more main clauses that are joined by a conjunction such as *and, so, or, but, because.*

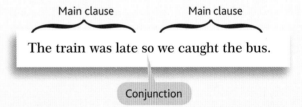

Complex sentences

These have one or more main clauses and one or more subordinate clauses. A subordinate clause does not make complete sense on its own. For example:

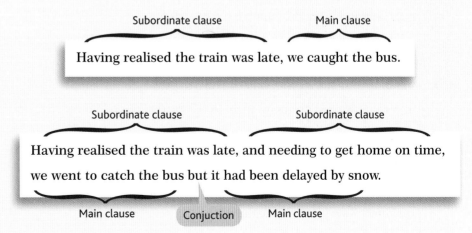

No one sentence type is better than another. There are times when a simple sentence is needed, perhaps for emphasis, and times when a compound or complex sentence is more appropriate. Read the following opening paragraph written by a student who was advising other students on things to do in the summer holidays to avoid boredom.

> *With the summer holidays fast approaching, the monotony of school soon over and the stress of exams shortly to be nothing more than a distant memory, it would not be unreasonable to expect that students feel some excitement or anticipation over their imminent freedom. Or would it?*

Top Tip

To demonstrate high-level control of sentence structures you need to be able to move freely between all three forms of sentences for maximum impact.

Notice how the student starts with a fully developed and controlled complex sentence and then deliberately follows this with a three-word rhetorical question for maximum effect.

Practice question

1 The following information about London is in simple sentences:

'London is the capital city of England. It is in south-east England. It has a population of about eight million people. It is the world's ninth-largest city. London is situated on the banks of the River Thames. The City of London is known as the Square Mile. It was the original settlement of the Romans. The Queen lives in Buckingham Palace in London.'

Experiment in building compound and complex sentences using the information given here. You can add or remove details if you wish. Your aim is to write a paragraph in which you demonstrate the ability to use a range of sentence structures for maximum effect.

2 When you have written your paragraph, use three different colours to highlight your simple, compound and complex sentences.

Varying word order

There are many different ways of expressing an idea. Varying the word order places different emphasis on different parts of a sentence. It also shows your examiner that you are in control of your words and where you place them.

Look at the variations on this sentence:

John walked down the street to the shop and then returned home.

Having walked down the street to the shop, John returned home.

John returned home, having walked down the street to the shop.

John, having walked down the street to the shop, returned home.

Practice question

3 Experiment with the following sentences to find out how many different ways you can write them:

- The little girl lost her doll in the park and cried all the way home.
- They met in an internet chat room and married three years later.
- The sales assistant asked the customers to leave immediately when the fire alarm rang.

Vocabulary

Using an ambitious vocabulary range is not about using long and complex words. It is about choosing words to have maximum impact on your reader.

Look at the following examples, which demonstrate how a few changes to vocabulary can greatly improve a sentence.

More than half of British children do not change the channel when it comes to adverts.

~~More than half~~ The majority of British children ~~do not~~ are reluctant to change the channel when ~~it comes to adverts~~ the adverts commence.

TV has to cut down on the adverts for sweets and change them to ones for fruit.

Potentially, TV ~~has to~~ could ~~cut down on~~ reduce the adverts for sweets and ~~change them to~~ substitute ones for fruit.

If your children have packed lunches, this is a chance for you to make fruit exciting for them by giving them lots of different kinds.

If your ~~children~~ little darlings have packed lunches, this is ~~a chance~~ a valuable opportunity for you to make fruit exciting for them by ~~giving~~ providing ~~them lots of different kinds~~ a varied and enticing range.

Practice question

4 Rewrite the following paragraph demonstrating a wider and more sophisticated and adult vocabulary range. In it a student writes about their sporting interest:

'My training routine and schedule would have to be tweaked quite a bit to match other leading professionals. School and college would be totally out of the question. I would have to become a full-time cyclist spending most of my spare time training. I would also need to improve my diet. At the moment, it's not very good and doesn't really give me enough energy to ride really fast.'

Highlight the words you have inserted. Do they demonstrate a more sophisticated and adult vocabulary range?

Top Tip

You do not need to use long complicated words – you do need to choose the words you use carefully to show you have a mature vocabulary range.

Phrasing

It is not just the words you choose which contribute to the assessment of your vocabulary usage. It is also the way that you use them.

Look at the following example:

> It's as though Government figures have been changed to make it look like people are richer than they are.

The sentence communicates clearly but could be much improved:

> It would appear that the Government figures have been massaged to create the impression of prosperity.

The words 'massaged' and 'prosperity' suggest a sophisticated vocabulary range. The phrases 'It would appear that' and 'to create an impression of', whilst containing relatively simple words, add to the impression of sophistication. This is written by a student who can choose which words to use for maximum impact.

Now look at alternative ways of expressing the same sentence:

> The evidence suggests that the Government figures have been massaged to create an illusion of prosperity.

> Perhaps the Government figures have been massaged to create an impression of prosperity?

> Government figures have, it would seem, been massaged to create a mirage of prosperity.

Top Tip

It is not just the words you use, it is the way you use them that gains you the highest marks.

Each of these alternatives demonstrates a mature sophisticated vocabulary range *and* fluent control of sentence structure.

Practice question

5 The sentences below each suggest a student with high-level skills. Experiment with rewriting them. You can change the vocabulary and the sentence structure in any way you want.

- It would seem that the elderly are becoming increasingly frightened of the youth of today.
- The rising crime rate is a direct consequence of fewer police on the streets.
- The media must take greater responsibility for the fear it creates.
- Young people today have nowhere to go to socialise and have fun.

Tone

The words you choose can also affect the tone of your writing. Tone is the writer's attitude towards the subject and the reader. It can be serious, comic, sarcastic, formal, angry, friendly, and so on.

Tone is created, in part, through vocabulary choice.

In the following example, the student creates a friendly, light-hearted tone. The features of the writing have been annotated for you.

Uses exaggeration

List to appeal to different readers

> *If by any chance you are creative, then it would be a crime not to express your creativity in whatever form it may take: the artist could produce a sensational landscape, the chef, a new and exciting recipe and, for the engineer, there is always the turbo charged Mechano windmill! Follow your interest and you can rest assured there will always be something for you to do.*

Addresses the reader directly

Uses humour

Uses language to put reader at ease

In the following example, the student creates a sarcastic tone, which leaves the reader in no doubt of their opinion. The features of the writing have been annotated for you.

Vocabulary to suggest celebration

Word that suggests contrast

Image to enhance meaning

> *The arrival of this new 'superstar' was heralded with fanfares and red carpets galore. Yet, when she arrived on stage, the trumpets stopped. With a screeching voice, which could halt schoolboys at five paces, she proceeded to torture her captive audience with tune after tuneless tune.*

Use of inverted commas to cast doubt on the word

Words to suggest pain

Repetitive play on words to emphasize point

Top Tip
You can influence your reader by adopting a specific tone.

6 Write the opening paragraphs of a letter to a local newspaper on a subject of interest to local readers. For example, it could be about:

- litter on the streets
- Christmas lights
- the types of shops in the local High Street
- local sports facilities.

Your aim is to create a sarcastic tone.

Now write the opening paragraphs of a letter on the same or a different subject. Your aim is to create a friendly tone.

Sentence structure and vocabulary

By using a range of sentence structures and sophisticated vocabulary and phrasing, a Grade C student can greatly improve their achievement.

Activity

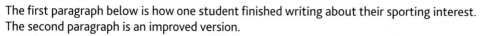

1 The first paragraph below is how one student finished writing about their sporting interest. The second paragraph is an improved version.

To help you identify the changes that have been made, copy and complete this table. The first line has been done for you:

First version	Improved version
To win this	Winning this
like	
gain respect	
and to gain respect	
an alpha male	
Along with all the respect	
to choose from	
The other thing that	
I would have been seen	
not just nationwide but worldwide	
That, with all the other things	
my total dream	

First version

To win this event is like to win a fight in a high school brawl. You gain respect off other riders and to gain respect in cycling is like being an alpha male in a lions' pride. Along with all the respect, you gain a vast variety of sponsorship deals to choose from. The other thing that would probably satisfy me the most would be that I would have been seen on television winning something not just nationwide but worldwide. That, with all the other things would make my total dream.

Improved version

Winning this event is comparable with winning a fight in a high school brawl. You gain respect and admiration from other riders and that, in cycling, is like being the alpha male in a lion's pride. Alongside respect, there are the sponsorship deals from which to choose. But there is one further desirable outcome: the event is televised. I would be watched by fascinated audiences across the globe. I would be famous. So, with respect, wealth and fame, I would have achieved my dream in its entirety.

Practice question

7 Write the opening paragraph of a text in which you explain what your dream for the future is. Aim to use a range of sentence structures and varied, sophisticated vocabulary and phrasing.

Look again at the examples above and then at your writing. Can you make further improvements to it?

Top Tip

Show your examiner that you can use a range of sentence structures.

Check your revision

- What do simple sentences always contain?
- What is the difference between a main clause and a subordinate clause?
- What is a compound sentence?
- What is a complex sentence?
- What kinds of sentence structures should you aim to use in your writing?
- What is your examiner looking for in your choices of vocabulary and phrasing?
- What is 'tone'? Suggest four different ways in which tone can be created.

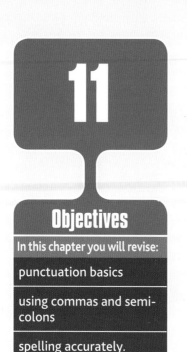

Technical accuracy

Technical accuracy in spelling and punctuation is important in an exam that assesses your writing skills in English. You need to draw together all that you have learnt about spelling and punctuation over 10 or 11 years to ensure that, on the day, your writing is as technically accurate as you can make it.

This chapter provides you with reminders of some of the basic rules and also emphasises some more sophisticated aspects of punctuation that will help you to gain a high grade.

Objectives

In this chapter you will revise:

punctuation basics

using commas and semi-colons

spelling accurately.

Punctuation basics

Capital letters

Capital letters are used at the start of a sentence and for:

- the personal pronoun *I*
- the first letter of proper nouns (people's names, place names, names of days and months) but not for the names of the seasons (spring, summer, etc.)
- the first letter of titles of people and organisations
- some abbreviations and acronyms (US, UNESCO)
- the main words in titles of books, films, etc. (*Lord of the Rings*).

Full stops

Full stops are used:

- to mark the end of a sentence
- sometimes to show abbreviations (B.Sc., e.g.).

Question marks

Question marks are used to:

- mark the end of a question.

Exclamation marks

Exclamation marks are used to:

- mark shouts or exclamations, or to show that something is entertaining or worthy of special note.

Apostrophes

Apostrophes are used to:

- show when one or more letters have been missed out (omission). The apostrophe is placed in the exact spot where the letter or letters that have been missed out would have been

we **are** → we're; I **would** → I'd

- show that something belongs to someone or something (possession).

my friend**'s** outfit

When the possessor is singular, as in the case of 'friend', the apostrophe is placed after the word and an 's' is added. When the possessor is plural and already ends in an 's' we just add an apostrophe.

my friend**s'** outfits.

When the possessor is plural but does not end in an 's' we add an apostrophe and an 's'.

the women**'s** homes.

Note and learn the following:
- 'Won't' means 'will not'.
- 'Shan't' means 'shall not'.
- The possessive words yours, his, hers, its, ours, whose and theirs are *not* written with an apostrophe.

Inverted commas

Inverted commas (sometimes referred to as speech marks or quotation marks) are used:

- when a writer uses a speaker's actual words

> "I'm sorry," said the receptionist, "but the doctor is busy."

- when a writer is quoting from another text.

> Larkin wrote this poem for a newborn girl whom he refers to as a "tightly-folded bud".

Colons

Colons are used to:
- introduce a list

> She packed a bag with the few items she owned: an old pair of jeans, two school shirts, a worn toothbrush and the precious photograph of her sister

- introduce a lengthy piece of direct speech or a quotation

> He looked her straight in the eye and said: 'This isn't easy for either of us. But we knew, when we started, there would be difficulties ahead.'

- introduce an idea for which the first part of the sentence has prepared the reader.

> The sermon, like so many others before it, contained only one message: do as I say, not as I do.

This may already seem like a lot to remember but these are punctuation marks you have been learning about for many years. Now, you need to make absolutely sure you can use them correctly.

Practice question

1 Rewrite the following sentences, using appropriate punctuation:
- kirsty and adam were the most unlikely couple they had met in cranehill secondary school and somehow managed to stay together when all their friends had gone in different directions they had always known their lives would be spent with each other
- this relatively easy walk on the crags above derwentwater in the lake district is quite spectacular early september is the best time for the heather though the great wood, currently owned by the national trust, is worth a visit at any time of year
- stop shouted the guard if you go any further, we will shoot you
- it was his first day at school and he needed to think carefully about what he should take the shiny lizard pencil case, his best batman cape, an apple and his brand-new laser fighter
- the warning was clear stop or be killed
- havent you got any more money he asked in a whisper
- no thats all there is weve spent everything else well just have to make do

1   Look back at the writing you have done for your English over the past few months and at the writing you have done in response to Activities in this book so far. Check that you have punctuated your writing accurately and correct any mistakes that you notice.

2   Note any common errors that you tend to make and give extra attention to getting these right in your examination.

Punctuation: advanced

Commas

Commas are used to:

● separate items in a list

> If you ever explore this area you will discover that you can go swimming, play football on the green or in the sports centre, visit a range of shops on the High Street and take advantage of the multiplex cinema.

● mark off extra information

> Mr Johnson, a father of four, was unable to show a receipt and Judge Christine Carr, sitting at Lincoln County Court, found him guilty of theft.

● separate a main clause from a subordinate clause

> Although the bus was late, he still got to school on time.

● mark off the spoken words in direct speech

> 'Come with me,' she whispered quietly to the crying child.

You may have wondered why commas did not appear on the previous page as you will have been learning about them for many years. It is important for you to know that, whilst many students can use commas correctly in a list, they often do not use them correctly to separate main and subordinate clauses. They also often use them when a full stop is needed.

Commas help the reader to follow the meaning of a text. Controlled and accurate use of commas is a sophisticated form of punctuation.

Top Tip

Examiners report that accurate use of commas within a sentence is often an indicator of a high-level candidate.

3   The following extracts are both written by professional writers. One is taken from the opening of a novel. The other is taken from a non-fiction article on travel. Read them aloud, pausing when you come across a full stop or a comma. Using the bullet points above to help you, work out why the commas are placed where they are.

> *I became what I am today at the age of twelve, on a frigid overcast day in the winter of 1975. I remember the precise moment, crouching behind a crumbling mud wall, peeking into the alley near the frozen creek. That was a long time ago, but it's wrong what they say about the past, I've learned, about how you can bury it. Because the past claws its way out. Looking back now, I realize I have been peeking into that deserted alley for the last twenty-six years.*
>
> Khaled Hosseini, *The Kite Runner*, 2004

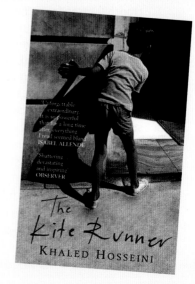

Activity cont'd

I was four when I went off travelling with my mother and elder sister, and six when we came back. For almost two years we wandered through Morocco. We rented small rooms in Medina hotels, hitchhiked, bartered, attended festivals and hammams, spoke Arabic and French. We ate the food they cooked in cauldrons in Marrakech, played with beggar children, befriended the women who sold drums. My sister went to a Moroccan school and learnt about the pillars of Islam, the laws by which the people lived their lives.

Esther Freud, 'How travel shaped my life', *The Traveller's Handbook*, 2008

Practice question

2 Read the following paragraph which is taken from the same article on travel as the above. The sentences are punctuated for you, but the commas have been left out. Read the paragraph aloud and decide where you should place commas to help the reader follow the meaning more easily.

Years later in my early twenties I started going to a creative writing class and after a series of assorted exercises we were set a task. Simply to write a longer piece. A five- or six-page piece about anything at all. What could I write about? I had no idea and then as soon as I sat down alone in a quiet room my stories all came back to me. Of course I'd write about the camel festival and cumin the beggar girls the drummer women in the square and although when I closed my eyes I could remember almost cinematically my life as it was then I realised I did have a head start. I'd practised these stories before.

Esther Freud, 'How travel shaped my life', *The Traveller's Handbook*, 2008

Semi-colons

Semi-colons are used to:

- separate items in a list, when the items are longer than usual

> The class raised the grand total by staging a wide range of events: a night-time sponsored walk in the Brecon Beacons; daily cake stalls throughout November; abseiling down the city-centre multi-storey car park; a penny trail round the four sides of the playing field; and, to the great delight of their parents, silent weekend sleepovers.

- take the place of a full stop between sentences that are closely linked in meaning.

> The first book was more interesting with tales of mystery and adventure; the second one was just plain boring.

It is the second of these uses that is both subtle and sophisticated. Students can sometimes overdo the use of the semi-colon and, in doing so, show they do not really understand how to use it. One semi-colon well placed is much more effective than five semi-colons randomly placed.

Activity

4 Look at a prose text which you have studied for controlled assessment or for your Literature. Reread a few pages and notice how the writer uses the semi-colon for effect.

5 Between now and your exam, whenever you are reading, be it a book, a magazine or a newspaper, make sure you notice when and how the writers use the semi-colon. The best way to learn is through good example.

Spelling: basic rules

Prefixes

A prefix is a group of letters that can be added to the beginning of a root word to change its meaning.

appear → disappear

Frequently used prefixes include:

re- mis- in- sub- im- anti- ir- dis-

Once you understand that the prefix is simply added on to the root word, it makes the spelling logical. 'Disappear' only has one 's' because 'dis' is added to 'appear'. 'Irresponsible' has two 'r's because 'ir' is added to 'responsible'.

Suffixes

A suffix is a letter or group of letters that can be added to the end of a root word to change its meaning.

appear → appear**ing**

Frequently used suffixes include:

-ly -able -ed -ful -ing -ment - ness -ity

In the vast majority of cases you simply add the suffix to the root word.

However, there are a few exceptions that you need to know. It looks like a long list but it is unlikely that you will come across anything here that you have not already been taught. The key is to remember the rules in the exam.

Exceptions	Examples
If the word ends in a *c*, add *k* when you add a suffix beginning with *e, i* or *y*.	picnic → picnicked
When adding the suffix *-ful* or *-ly* to words that end in a consonant followed by *y*, change the *y* to *i*	plenty → plentiful happy → happily
When a suffix begins with a vowel and the root word ends in e, drop the e.	write → writing fame → famous
When a suffix begins with a vowel and the root word ends in *ee, oe* or *ye*, you keep the final *e*.	agree → agreeable canoe → canoeing
When you add the suffix *able* to a root word that ends in *ce* or *ge* you keep the final *e*.	notice → noticeable change → changeable
Consonants are usually doubled when you add *-ar,-er, -ed* or *-ing* to a word that has one syllable and ends with a short vowel and any consonant **except** *y* or *x*.	run → running, beg → beggar play → playing tax → taxed

Understanding how prefixes and suffixes work helps you to be more accurate in your spelling. So, for example, if you can spell 'satisfy' correctly you should also be able to spell 'dissatisfied', 'unsatisfactory', 'satisfaction' and 'satisfying'.

Activity

6   Use the chart below to help you make as many words as you can using the root words, a prefix and one or more suffixes.

Prefix	Root word	Suffix
re	agree	able
in	fair	ment
sub	reverse	ly
im	sense	ed
anti	perfect	ful
ir	skill	ing
dis	success	ion
un	honest	ible
	satisfy	less

Plurals

Plural means more than one.

For the vast majority of plural forms you simply add 's' to the singular forms.

book → books   computer → computers

There are some exceptions that you need to learn.

Exceptions	Examples
When the singular form ends in -s, -x, -ch or -sh, add es.	bus → buses tax → taxes church → churches flash → flashes
If a word ends in -y and has a consonant before the last letter, change the y to an i and add es.	party → parties fly → flies
If a word ends in -o you usually just add s. However, there are a few commonly used words that need es to make them plural.	tomato → tomatoes potato → potatoes hero → heroes
If a word ends in -f or -fe you usually change the -f or -fe to –ves.	wolf → wolves knife → knives
But there are a few exceptions to the previous rule.	roof → roofs chief → chiefs reef → reefs

There are also some irregular plurals, many of which you will already know. Here are some examples of them:

child → children   man → men   formula → formulae

sheep → sheep   mouse → mice   crisis → crises

tooth → teeth   person → people   stimulus → stimuli

3 Using the above rules, write the plurals of the following words. There are a few irregular words included in the list:

lunch Monday Christmas beach radius lady atlas inch woman blush comedy cactus takeaway hoax stitch ferry bonus plus essay gas arch coach key wish blotch bully doorman hippopotamus medium scissors

Homonyms

Homonyms are words that have the same spelling *or* pronunciation as another, but a different meaning or origin. Students often get confused with homonyms that have a different spelling and a different meaning but that sound the same. Here are some of the homonyms that students frequently mix up.

Top Tip

Always read through your writing and correct errors in punctuation and spelling.

peace/piece   where/were/wear/we're   their/there/they're

pair/pear   profit/prophet   allowed/aloud   hole/whole

bough/bow   great/grate   ceiling/sealing

4 Choose the correct word to fill the spaces in the following sentences:

- (Where/Were/Wear/We're) going into town (where/were/wear/we're) we are hoping to find something new to (where/were/wear/we're) to the wedding.
- The (profit/prophet) said he would bring (peace/piece) to the land.
- The (hole/whole) of the (great/grate) hall, including the (ceiling/sealing), was bathed in sunshine.
- (Their/There/They're) not (allowed/aloud) to go in (their/there/they're) until (their/there/they're) muddy boots are removed.

Check your revision

Answer the following questions to make sure you have understood the work in this chapter:

- For which two reasons would you use inverted commas?
- What are the abbreviated forms of 'will not' and 'shall not'?
- Complete this sentence: The correct use of _____ within a piece of extended writing is often an indicator of a more able student.
- Complete this sentence: One semi-colon _____ is much more effective than five semi-colons _____.
- What are prefixes and suffixes?
- Write the plurals of the following words: sheep, crisis, tomato, roof, taxi, fly.

Key terms

Cohesive text: a piece of writing in which the parts are closely connected to each other.

How to gain the highest grades

So far we have examined the features of good writing, which include:

- answering the question in a planned and organised way
- engaging the reader by using a range of techniques
- using a varied range of sentence structures for effect
- using a sophisticated and adult vocabulary
- achieving a high level of technical accuracy.

All of these things combined will help you to achieve a high grade in your writing. However, there are two more features which define the very best types of writing. The first of these is the ability to write fluently.

Writing fluently

The ability to write fluently means that the writer has created a **cohesive text** – a piece of writing that has internal links both within and between paragraphs. In order to achieve this, the writer must have a sound grasp of the bigger picture: at each stage of writing they must maintain awareness of where they have been and where they are going.

The first piece of writing that you will examine was written in response to a shorter writing task. The student was awarded a mark at the bottom of the A band and was addressing this task:

> Write a letter to a national newspaper in which you argue that we must do more to protect our environment.

Read the letter before completing the activities relating to it.

People of Britain,

Listen up! We all share a beautiful and complex world which is well designed and works like an amazing machine, whirring and turning all day long and keeping millions of people alive. If the lifetime of our planet earth was like a day, we humans have been on it for just a minute. And yet in our minute a red rust has formed over the machine, covering the shiny steel, and destroying the screws which hold it together. The machine is overheating and almost at melting point. Soon it might stop altogether.

Extreme? Maybe. But the truth is that we have dramatically changed this planet and not for the better. With our landfill sites and our smoking cities, we are seriously damaging the engine that has kept our world going for millions of years. It's mind boggling just how much power we have. But, with power comes responsibility. The time has come for us to learn how our machine works and to begin to mend the damage we have done to it. We have to wipe away the rust and oil the screws so that we make things better for us and for our children and for their children too. We have the power to make the future better or worse. We should take this power with both hands and use it wisely.

We must start today by cutting down on the energy we use both at home and at work. We've got to stop so many planes flying and make sure that the rain forests are not destroyed. We've got to make our politicians listen to us and make them do things. As individuals we have to do things too. We should turn off lights, stop wasting water, walk rather than take the car and make sure we recycle anything we can. Everything we do matters, so let's make the effort now so that our children will still see the sun rise.

Oliver Redmund, Liverpool

Activity

1. The student uses the first-person plural pronouns, we and our, as a means of including the reader and creating text coherence. Count or highlight the number of times these terms appear.

2. The student makes close links between one paragraph and the next. Look at the following table which shows the endings and openings of consecutive paragraphs. For each one, explain how a link is made.

1st paragraph ending: Soon it might stop altogether.	2nd paragraph opening: Extreme?
2nd paragraph ending: But, with power comes responsibility.	3rd paragraph opening: The time has come for us to …
3rd paragraph ending: We who should take this power with both hands and use it wisely	4th paragraph opening: We must start today by …

3. The student uses the image of the machine to provide whole text coherence. For each paragraph, list the references to the machine.

Top Tip

To write fluently you need to make clear links within and between paragraphs.

Practice question

1 Write a letter to a national newspaper in which you argue for better training opportunities for young people today.

Aim to produce a cohesive text by:

- regular and consistent use of pronouns
- effective linking between paragraphs
- use of a recurrent image such as the cultivation of a plant or the creation of a work of art.

Letter layout

The student above was asked to write a letter to a newspaper. Such letters are often sent by email and generally, in these cases, you just need to provide the greeting, the body of the letter and an appropriate ending and signature. Sometimes, however, you may be asked to write a letter to be sent by post, perhaps to a particular business, or a politician, or to the Chair of Governors at your school. Use this template to help you set your letter out appropriately.

Writer's full address and postcode. You do not have to use punctuation. If you do, you should be consistent, placing a comma at the end of each line until the last which should have a full stop before the postcode

The day's date in full

Name (if known), title and address of the intended recipient

Greeting: Dear Sir, Dear Madam or Dear Mr, Ms, Mrs or Miss, followed by the person's surname

Body of the letter with ideas organised into paragraphs

Ending: Yours sincerely (if the recipient is addressed by name), Yours faithfully (if not).

Signature of writer. If the signature is difficult to read, the writer's name should be printed below it

Always read the task carefully to make sure you are doing exactly what you have been asked to do.

Practice question

2 Study the template for a formal letter. Then, close this book and sketch your own copy of it from memory. Annotate the different parts. You should annotate seven different elements. When you have finished, check your template to make sure you know how to set out a formal letter.

Writing with a distinctive individual voice

In the letter on page 80 the student maintained a consistent personal voice. This allows the reader to develop a clear sense of the writer. Sometimes a student will use their own 'voice'. On occasions, a student might adopt a voice. For example, by choosing to write as a parent or a business person, depending on the task. The student whose writing is on the opposite page was responding to this longer writing task:

Write an informative article for teachers about the importance of clothes to today's teenagers.

Activity

4 Read the student's response to the above task. What 'voice' do they adopt? Find evidence from different parts of the response to show that the student sustains this 'voice'.

5 This student achieved full marks for their writing. Read the response and, as you read, list the qualities of the writing that you think led to the award of full marks. These may be to do with both content and writing style.

6 Record your comments in a table like this:

Qualities of writing	Example

Clothes and today's teenagers

Sick and tired of telling them to tuck their shirts in? Shocked by what they wear? Read on …

What the government often don't realise is that there's much more to being a teacher than teaching. We act as counsellors, nursemaids, disciplinarians and, more often than not, the fashion police.

In order for teachers to deal with the problems of bared midriffs, towering heels and untied ties, they need first to understand what drives our teenagers to go for that 'just-got-out-of-bed' or 'just-been-out-all-night' look. Cast your minds back to your teenage years (if that's hard, you'll begin to understand why younger teachers have fewer problems with uniform). If you wore, at some stage, ra-ra skirts, leg-warmers or flares, you can hardly blame your current pupils. Sad to say, but what drove most of us then, still drives them today – fashion.

The teenage years are nearly always rocky ones. Spots, greasy hair and physical development only make them worse. To make up for this, many teenagers use their growing independence to kit themselves out with the latest gear – you can't help acne but you can help what you wear and how you wear it.

Today, fashion dictates what's in the shops and hence what will be worn. Being fashionable is about being in with the in-crowd and, for a teenager, not being 'in' can be a major worry. If it means flouting pale limbs in shoe-string tops in February, it will be done. Thus, teachers should be more aware, and perhaps more tolerant, of the not-so-pretty-and-popular kids who feel they can repair some of the damage with trendy clothes.

Just as for teachers who power-dress or those who wear T-shirts and jeans to 'connect with the kids', teenagers use clothes to create an image for themselves. They also use clothes as a means of identifying with a particular social group. With our modern media, society as a whole revolves around appearance and teenagers are the early victims of this preoccupation. It's not their fault – who built this society?

It would be helpful if teachers could at least try to understand what's in fashion and why teenagers follow it. Whether it's military style, Goth, Emo or Romantic, there's a reason for it. Empathy is the key both to accepting your pupils' values and to winning their respect. I am not condoning unsuitable clothing in school, just recommending tolerance. And, before you say anything at all, you might just want to find out what they think of what you're wearing!

7 Now look at the list of features below credited by the examiner. How many of these did you spot? You may not have used the same words as the examiner.

- Shows clarity of thought.
- Communicates in a convincing way.
- Engages the reader directly.
- Offers a range of relevant, interesting information.
- Uses an appropriate tone to influence the reader.
- Makes effective use of rhetorical devices.
- Uses paragraphs emphasise meaning.
- Presents complex and challenging ideas.
- Shows varied use of sentence structures.
- Punctuates complex structures accurately.
- Spells complex words accurately.
- Shows originality and ambition.

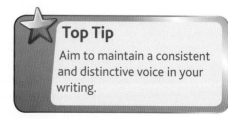

Top Tip

Aim to maintain a consistent and distinctive voice in your writing.

Practice question

3 Carry out the following task: Write an informative article for young people about the importance of looking after the elderly.

Experiment with adopting a voice other than your own. It could, for example, be a pensioner's voice. Aim to spend about 35 minutes on planning and writing your response.

Check your own writing against the examiner's list above. How many of the bullet points have you achieved?

Check your revision

In Chapter 13 you are going to look at exam questions and how different students have responded to them. At different times you will be asked to act as the expert and to make judgements on the quality of the writing. Before you start Chapter 13, look back over all the work you have revised on writing, including the practice pieces that you have done. Remind yourself of the different areas you have covered and make a list of them. If there are any of these areas that you are not sure about, reread the relevant chapter.

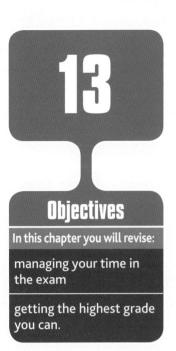

13

Objectives

In this chapter you will revise:

managing your time in the exam

getting the highest grade you can.

Making your writing skills count in the exam

 In Section B, the writing part of your exam, you will be asked to complete two writing tasks: one shorter task worth 16 marks and one longer task worth 24 marks.

You have one hour to complete the Writing section … one hour in which to demonstrate all the skills you have accumulated in writing. In order to ensure you get as many marks as possible, you need to complete both pieces of writing. A sensible time guide would be:

Shorter writing task = 25 minutes

Longer writing task = 35 minutes

If you allow 4–5 minutes' planning for each piece, this then gives you 20 minutes to write your first answer and 30 minutes to write your second one. Plan to write 3–4 paragraphs for the shorter writing task and 4–5 paragraphs for the longer one. Remember, there is no point doing one task really well and then failing to do the second one.

Before you continue, look back to page 51 and remind yourself of the skills on which you will be tested. You will be tested on all parts of the Assessment Objectives in each question.

In this section you are going to read and assess different responses to two exam questions. You should use what you learn about the achievements of other students to help you do your best in your own writing in the exam.

Top Tip

Watch the clock and keep to strict time schedules so that you pick up marks for both writing tasks.

Shorter writing task

The piece on the following page was written by a student in response to the following shorter writing task. It was placed in the Grade C band.

> Write a letter to be sent by post to the Prime Minister in which you suggest ways of improving your local area or the country.
>
> (*16 marks*)

Activity

1. Read the student's answer to this short writing task.

2. Assess the student's response using the following criteria based on the Assessment Objectives:
   - The student communicates his ideas with *some success/clearly/convincingly*.
   - He engages the reader with *some linked information/detailed information*.
   - His tone is *sometimes/always* appropriate and *affects/manipulates* the reader's response.
   - He uses devices such as rhetorical questions and repetition for effect *rarely/effectively/very effectively*.
   - His range of vocabulary is *limited/varied/mature and sophisticated*.
   - He uses paragraphs *sometimes/always to enhance meaning*.
   - His use of sentence structures is *limited/varied/effective*.
   - His spelling and punctuation are *sometimes/usually/mostly accurate*.

3. Choose two areas where you think the student most needs to improve in order to get a higher grade, and set the student two targets.

Student 1

Dear Prime Minister,

I am writing to you on behalf of the general public. Over the past few years I have noticed that our country is going downhill, and I just wanted to give you a nudge in the right direction as to what to do. I'm sure every member of the public have their own says of what's right and wrong, but I'm going to get across to you what I think would make a better country.

I'll start with youthism. I think that in the 21st century the elders of the public seem to dispise the members of the younger public and label them all as hoodies and druggies and other vile names. But I believe that if we changed this little thing, then, well things could get better. Think of it as laying a foundation. You could start small by just building youth centres or fully using the ones which are already available.

There are a few other things that bother me. I'll start with the lack of police which is quite simply causing everything to go pear-shaped. As new laws have been introduced, the number of gun crimes and street crimes has increased. The way the police force is run is outrageous, when an elderly lady rings at stupid o'clock saying there's drunk and disorderly children outside her house they should be responding immediately but that just isn't happening.

Just before I finish my letter I just quickly want to say that the quality of public transport is a disgrace and far too over price. Plus if it's cheaper to get on a train or bus, more people will use one, therefore cutting the CO2 emmisions. If you correct all these faults I believe that our country could be better and could be one of the higher countrys in the continent of Europe.

Thank you,
Yours sincerely,
Daryl Casey

Activity

4   Now read the examiner's comments on the student's writing and the targets that the examiner set. Did you identify similar strengths and weaknesses?

Examiner comments:

What the student does

The student writes for audience and purpose, and the detail is logically sequenced. He communicates clearly most of the time and the tone is usually appropriate though at times it slips into informality. Ideas are organised into sentences and paragraphs. The vocabulary is relatively simple though the student is beginning to use some more complex words, such as 'outrageous'. Capital letters and full stops are used correctly and there is occasionally correct use of commas.

What the student needs to do to improve

Careful planning would ensure each paragraph had a clear focus. Standard English should be used throughout; terms such as 'have their own says' and 'stupid o'clock' are not appropriate. The candidate should focus on developing a wider vocabulary range with more mature phrasing.

Activity

5 Now read the following response to the same task. It is much better. The student was awarded a mark in the Grade A band.

6 Using the same assessment criteria as you used in Activity 2, identify ways in which this student's writing is better than that of student 1.

7 Write the examiner's comments on this piece of writing.

Student 2

11 Seacombe Tce
Brightholme
WJ24 5EX

The Prime Minister   21st May, 2010
The Houses of Parliament
Westminster

Dear Prime Minister,

The return from a holiday is always a depressing experience, but when one is coming home to England, it is even more so. Having recently spent a glorious fortnight in France, it was with grim faces and sad hearts that we viewed once more the well known cliffs of Dover.

Whilst it would be unreasonable to expect you to do anything about the weather, it does seem there is much you could do to improve England's appeal. At present the government appears to have sunk into meltdown, with details of the actions of unscrupulous MPs becoming more and more sordid by the day. Frankly, a shack on the surface of Mars would seem a more attractive prospect than living in England at the moment. Surely you could do something to improve this situation and make our representatives worthy of that title?

It's not just the MPs who seem to be acting in a dishonest manner. The bankers also have much to answer for. Having lost millions, if not billions, of our money they still want bonuses and think they have a right to them. They argue they are needed to keep the best people in the banks but I ask you: Would we be in this mess if we had the best people running our banks? I don't think so. It's time for you to tell them we've all had enough.

With honesty back at the heart of government and the banks firmly under control, people would have more confidence again and would be more prepared to believe what they are told. Who knows? The view from the ferry might even be a sunny one after all!

Yours faithfully,
Matthew Patel

(A)

Longer writing task

The piece below was written by a student in response to the following longer writing task. The answer was placed in the Grade B band.

Write an article for your school website in which you argue that life is, or is not, too stressful for teenagers nowadays. *(24 marks)*

Activity

8 Complete the first column of the chart by identifying and listing three positive features of the student's writing that you think helped them to achieve a Grade B. Complete the second column by listing two negative features of the writing that you think prevented them from getting a higher grade. You could use the Assessment Objectives on page 51 to help you. Set two targets that you think will help the student to get a higher grade.

Things the student does well	Things the student does not do well
Targets	
1	
2	

Student 3

In my eyes the main pressures on young people today really make life stressful for teenagers nowadays. If it isn't bullying or your parents nagging you, it's school and teachers and exams. Also revision gets you stressed because you think you're revising all the wrong things or you're scared that you're not going to remember everything. Young people today just can't win.

Another pressure is popularity. If you're not popular then you're nothing. People will walk all over you, bully you and not even notice you most of the time unless they want a laugh or your dinner money.

Another stress that we have as the younger generation is ... yes, you've guessed it – money. As the saying goes, 'Money makes the world go round' and without it – well, boredom strikes yet again.

The pressure of all pressures though has to be exams. School work is getting more challenging and teachers from every subject are wanting us to 'work harder' and focus on that subject. Parents too are terrorising us to buckle down and concentrate more. All eyes are on us. We are forever reminded of how important and life changing our results can be; colleges are expecting strings of A and A* grades from each and every one of us. For those of us who are not academic, this is all but impossible, these periods just cause stress and anger which we may indeed take out on fellow siblings and adults; giving us this stereotypical image – but who can blame us?

One of my friends has been taken over by her mother. Her mother never lets her out of the house because she has to revise and study for her exams. But I mean, you need a break, you can't work all day and all night because then the information stops being useful and becomes a foreign language and just makes your brain switch off.

Parents say they understand what young people are going through but they don't. Life for a teenager today is very stressful.

Activity

9 Now read the examiner's comments on the student's work. Did you set the student similar targets to those set by the examiner?

Examiner comments:

What the student does

The writing is organised into sentences and paragraphs and the student matches the writing to purpose and audience most of the time. Whilst there is some variety in sentence structures, they are not always grammatically secure. The student begins to use more mature vocabulary with words such as 'terrorising' and more mature phrasing, for example 'from each and every one of us'. Spelling is generally accurate. There is some range in punctuation though the student is not secure in the accurate use of commas.

What the student needs to do to improve

The student needs to plan the content of each paragraph more carefully before starting to write. This would help the student to vary the paragraph openings and make them less repetitive. The student should aim to show a wider, more adult vocabulary range and the ability to structure complex sentences using commas correctly.

10 Now read the following response to the same task. It is much better. This student was awarded a mark in the Grade A* band.

11 Using the same assessment criteria as you used in Activity 2, identify the ways in which this student's writing is better than that of the previous student.

12 List the ways in which this piece of writing is better than that of the previous student. For each feature which you list, select an example from the writing. You could record your findings in a table like the one below.

High-level feature of writing	Example
Avoids repeating question in opening sentence	In today's ....differently.
Establishes personal relationship with reader	You see, my brain ... but to me it is.

Student 4

In today's fast-moving world, there are more pressures on young people than perhaps any previous generation and, of course, everyone reacts to these very differently. I am a good example of this. You see, my brain is faulty in that it cannot handle stress. It is not an official disability, of course, but to me it is. I am sixteen years old and sometimes I feel close to a nervous breakdown due to the pressures of being a teenager in today's world.

The first and foremost source of stress is school. School, more than anything else, piles on the pressures at every stage. There is not only the work aspect of it – there are social repercussions. Nothing, in my humble opinion, will ruin a young boy's chances in life more than being called 'spotty' or 'shorty' on the first day of school. And, assuming those early days are survived, the smallest blip, the tiniest foul-up will see 'spotty, snotty Matthews' picked on for months. Childish, yes, insignificant, maybe, but to an eleven-year-old student, heart-breaking. We now recall that I have not even started on work.

They try to keep the pressure off, obviously, but it is impossible to do so when the brave teacher must stand in front of 250 gawping children and admit, 'Now, these exams, um, now you know you can only do your best and they're really not important but they will decide the rest of your life. But don't worry.'

Thanks.

So, where better for the stressed teenager to relax after a hard day's work than in the comfort of his or her family home? Anywhere, actually, for in the 21st century, home is where the Hell is. Those parents who are not already divorced soon will be and the few children who are lucky enough to have a functional family know this. Divorce is at an all-time high and marriage is no longer sacred. The youth of today must endure the breakdown of this institution and do not have much to look forward to. However, the problems at home can be avoided; I, like many others, spend as little time there as possible.

These are just a few of the pressures under which we 'young uns' sink or swim. Add to these the hopelessness of adolescent hormones, the agony of finding 'true love' only to be dumped the next week, and the argument is unquestionably won. Too stressful nowadays? Of course. Too stressful to survive? Let's wait and see.

Check your revision

Below you will find the main skills that examiners look for in a student's writing in order to award an A or A* grade. Look back at the writing of Students 2 and 4. Try to identify some or all of these skills in their writing.

Communication

Shows clarity of thought.

Communication is convincing and compelling.

Engages reader with detailed and developed ideas.

Targets purpose in a sustained and focused way.

Adopts an appropriate tone.

Uses a range of language features in an effective way.

Integrates **discursive markers**.

Organisation

Continuous prose is used.

Paragraphs are used effectively.

Ideas are linked fluently.

Complex ideas are presented in a coherent way.

Sentence structure, spelling and punctuation

A variety of sentence structures is used to influence the reader.

Punctuation within and between sentences is effective.

Complex words are spelt accurately.

Key terms

Discursive markers: words or phrases used to help structure and develop the content, for example: in a similar way; nevertheless; although.

14

Practice examination for the writing section

Here are two questions, typical of the exam you will take. Both questions test the full range of skills. The marks awarded for each answer are also indicated.

> Write a letter to a relative who lives in a different place from you, inviting him or her to visit your home and informing him or her of the different things you could do in your area. *(16 marks)*
>
> Some people believe that education should only be made available to those who are prepared to make good use of it. Write an article for a teachers' magazine which argues for or against this idea. *(24 marks)*

You should divide your time according to the number of marks awarded to both tasks. As a rough guide, allow 25 minutes for the first task and 35 minutes for the second task.

Remember:

1   Read the questions closely and highlight key words. Make sure you know the subject, purpose, audience and form. Remember, as well as the stated audience, you are always writing for an examiner.

2   Spend up to five minutes planning. Gather a range of ideas and decide on the order in which you are going to write about them. Be in control of your writing.

3   Remind yourself of the high-level skills you need to demonstrate in your writing.

4   Do not repeat the question in your opening sentence. Aim to start in an interesting way that will grab your reader's attention.

5   Write in paragraphs and make fluent links within and between them.

6   After each paragraph, stop and read what you have written. Make sure it communicates clearly and that you are still addressing the question.

7   Aim to use a range of sentence structures to make your writing lively and interesting.

8   Aim to use a range of mature and sophisticated vocabulary and phrasing.

9   Keep an eye on the clock so that you have time to complete both writing tasks.

10   Check your writing closely. Read it 'aloud' in your head. Correct any errors that you spot in punctuation and spelling, and make any other improvements.

Take a deep breath and relax, knowing you have done your best!

Answers

Chapter 1: Analysing advertisements

Reading with understanding

Activity 1

Any four of the following:

- Experience the city's restaurants, shops and cultural attractions.
- Jump on a ferry to nearby islands.
- Take a day trip to the mountains or the rainforests.
- Journey east to the high desert and wine regions.

Activity 2

a   Something different and exciting.

b   Wide range of contrasting things to do – likely to have wide appeal.

c   Range of places to be explored, e.g. islands, mountains; unusual places, e.g. rainforests, high desert; sounds active, e.g. jump, journey east.

d   Shows the contrasts through examples, e.g. shops/mountains.

Commenting on structure and presentation

Activity 5

Heading, photograph, detail about Seattle, detail about www.ExperienceWA.com

Activity 6

The likely choice is the photograph – the eye is generally drawn to the centre of a text. The photograph, with its contrast between the city and the mountain in the background, would appeal to possible visitors.

Activity 7

The likely choice is the detail about www.ExperienceWA.com – functional information is often given at the end of a text for readers who want to find out more.

Thinking about language

Practice 3

Feature of language use	Example(s) of feature	Comment on feature
Addresses reader directly	'your Washington State adventure', 'your exploration', 'your journey'	Involves the reader – makes the text feel personal to them – helps them to anticipate actually going there and doing these things.
Directives (also known as imperatives and command verbs)	'experience', 'jump', 'take', 'journey'	Very direct (as compared with 'you could …'). Suggests that these things are easily done and makes a direct link with the reader.
Present tense	'Seattle is', 'we also make'	Creates a sense of immediacy – you can do these things now, today.

Evaluating effectiveness

Activities 8 and 9

All the given purposes and audiences are valid. The choice of rank order will depend on your interpretation of the text.

- To inform the reader about Seattle, e.g. over 25 international flights arriving regularly.
- To advise the reader about what to do in Seattle, e.g. Take a day trip to ….
- To persuade the reader to go to Seattle, e.g. the perfect mix of experiences.

- To persuade the reader to find out more about Seattle, e.g. contact our local representative.
- To advertise Seattle as a tourist destination, e.g. Washington State Tourism.

Activity 10
- People who want a quiet holiday, e.g. nearby islands.
- People who intend to visit the Pacific Northwest, e.g. gateway to begin your exploration.
- People seeking a holiday in the US, e.g. those from the UK.
- People who want a holiday that offers a range of activities, e.g. the perfect mix.
- People interested in setting up business in Seattle, e.g. industrious.

Check your revision

Reading with understanding
What does the advert suggest a visitor can do in Washington State?
- Experience a unique place – UNESCO World Heritage Site and an International Biosphere Reserve, a mystical world.
- Experience nature – lush, green, quiet, moss-covered.
- Be active – hike, bike, raft or kayak.
- Explore – 70 miles of rugged coastline.

Commenting on structure and presentation
Predominance of colour green – colour associated with nature and outdoors – reinforces outdoor activities such as walking and kayaking – also echoes of the Green Movement – reflecting heading – illustrates the word 'lush' – light through trees adds mystery and sense of enchantment.

Thinking about language
The adjectives include: mystical, lush, green, quiet, moss-covered, fresh-scented, primeval, rugged, boundless. Aim to pick a few of these and analyse in detail, e.g.:

> The use of 'primeval' suggests the early ages of the world and a time lost to history. This reinforces the notion of rarity and beauty as though the reader is being given the chance to explore an area that few people ever experience. This image is also projected in the word 'rugged', which suggests the coastline is in its natural state and has not been tampered with by mankind.

Evaluating effectiveness
Points you could have made include:
- Central image of rain forest effectively illustrates written text; predominant use of green links with and gives emphasis to the word play in the title; four-part structure means you progress through the advert in stages, each part leading you into the next part; white font is distinctive and easy to read.
- Criticisms are also valid, providing they are supported, e.g.:

> The use of green, whilst echoing the theme of the advert, is overdone and greater variation in colour may well have resulted in a more dynamic and appealing advertisement.

Chapter 2: Reading reviews

Thinking about tone

Activity 3
a humorous/affectionate
b enthusiastic/amused
c concerned/serious
d critical/sarcastic
e enthusiastic/affectionate
f enthusiastic/concerned

Activity 4

a   The writer seems to want to convey his enthusiasm to his reader.

b   The writer seems to like and be recommending the book, though he sometimes gives the impression that he thinks the photos are too perfect.

c   The writer seems to feel both admiration and concern for the Omo tribes.

Investigating language

Activity 5

Green: points about language

Yellow: comments on purpose

The subheading starts with the directive 'Venture into'. Here the writer immediately addresses the reader directly and the word 'venture' with its echoes of 'adventure' suggests this might be an exciting thing to do. Personal pronouns are used to involve the reader and anticipate his or her likely response to the book: 'leaving you wondering'; 'you'll be entranced by'. This helps to make the writing feel personal to the specific reader rather than the general public. Added to this the writer uses pronouns to put herself on the same side as the reader: 'And we're not talking …'; 'our eyes'. By doing this the intention is to draw the reader in and make the reader feel as though the writer understands his or her needs and has similar ones.

Commenting on structure and presentation

Activity 8

a   The 'true' in the headline has a double meaning – it suggests this is a real tribe and not one created by fashion, and also that they are a genuine and authentic people. The meaning becomes clear by the end of the second paragraph.

b   In the third paragraph.

c   1e, 2g, 3a, 4b, 5f, 6c, 7d.

Evaluating effectiveness

Activity 9

The following purposes are valid choices:

a   To inform the reader about the Omo people, e.g. 'Ethiopia's isolated Omo Valley'.

b   To inform the reader about the book *Natural Fashion*, e.g. 'His latest tome …'.

c   To advise the reader to read a particular book, e.g. 'You'll be entranced by …'.

e   To reveal the writer's opinion of a particular book, e.g. 'visual spectacle'.

Activity 10

The following audiences are valid choices:

b   Adults who want to learn about Ethiopia, e.g. 'Ethiopia's isolated Omo Valley'.

c   Adults interested in art and photography, e.g. 'some of the portraits'.

d   People interested in learning about other cultures, e.g. 'But this is an intrinsic part of their culture …'.

The rank orders chosen for b and d may vary.

Check your revision

Exploring meaning

dove – plunged into

unscathed – without hurt or damage

slew – great number of

Thinking about tone

Individual choices are valid providing they are supported by example.

Investigating language

Points could include: writes from first person perspective to emphasise personal experience of and response to the game – also encourages reader to identify with writer and her experiences and opinions; addresses reader directly – builds a more personal relationship with the reader – helps reader to visualise themself playing the game.

Commenting on structure and presentation

Points could include:

Visually review is structured in distinct parts, i.e. Title and sub-title, images, written text, additional image at bottom left to make text more cohesive.

Written text moves reader from low expectations of game to high expectations. Gives detailed description of game to support claim to have found new obsession made at the end of the first paragraph. Extended list used in third paragraph as a means of conveying the full range of attractions concisely.

Evaluating effectiveness

Areas you could have developed comments on include:

Designed to persuade; uses technical language, e.g. analog, multiplier – targeting readers who know about games; uses language informally, e.g. 'I'll be honest …', and 'oh boy …'; uses adjectives to describe, e.g. delicate, strategic balance, zombie zapping pad.

Comments should be focused on how effective you found the language to be and the reasons for your judgements.

Chapter 3: Making comparisons

What is the question?

Practice 1

- How is language used for effect in Item 1? Compare this with the way language is used for effect in Item 2. Examine some examples from both items and explain what their effects are.
- Compare the methods used in Item 1 and Item 2 to make the text appeal to the reader. Examine some examples and explain what the effects are.
- Compare how language is used to influence the intended audience in Item 1 and Item 2. Examine some examples and explain what the effects are.
- Examine some examples of the ways in which presentational and structural devices are used for effect in Item 1. Compare these with examples of how presentational and structural devices are used for effect in Item 2.

Making choices

Activity 1

Feature of language use in Item 1.1	Example(s) of feature	Feature of language use in Item 2.1	Example(s) of feature
Phrases containing contrasts	'cosmopolitan and casual' 'urban and natural' 'industrious and playful'	Addresses reader directly	'Venture into' 'leaving you wondering' 'you'll be entranced by'
Addresses reader directly	'your Washington State adventure' 'your exploration' 'your journey'	Lists	'collecting water, herding goats and … getting dressed up' 'the Omo's men, women and children' 'costumes, makeup and elaborate headgear'
Directives	'experience' 'jump' 'take' 'journey'	Sophisticated vocabulary	'guerrilla warfare is commonplace' 'their penchant for body adornment' 'exquisitely styled'
Present tense	'Seattle is' 'It's all here' 'we also make'	Vocabulary to persuade	'dazzling portraits' 'so exquisitely styled' 'impossible not to marvel at the visual spectacle
Vocabulary to persuade	'perfect gateway' 'renowned restaurants'	Present tense	'Dawn breaks' 'His latest tome is bursting …' 'it's impossible not to …'

Writing an answer

Activity 2

refers to text

inference

analysis

refers to text

refers to text

refers to text

similarity/ refers
to text

refers to text

purpose and audience

inference

> The writers of both texts share a technique in
> common: they both address the reader directly
> through the use of directives and personal pronouns.
> In Item 1.1 the reader is directed to 'experience', 'jump',
> 'take' and 'journey'. These verbs all suggest action
> and movement, successfully reinforcing the notion
> that there is much to do in Seattle and mirroring
> the implication of the earlier phrase 'industrious and
> playful'. The writer of Item 2.1 makes more limited use
> of directives though the one that is used is placed in a
> strategic position. At the start of the sub-heading the
> reader is directed to 'Venture into', the word 'venture'
> with its echoes of 'adventure' suggests this will be an
> exciting thing to do.
> Personal pronouns are used by both writers. Item
> 1.1 writer refers to 'your Washington State adventure',
> 'your journey', targeting the reader and making them
> feel as though the text is personally directed to them.
> Similarly, in Item 2.1 we find 'leaving you wondering'
> and 'you'll be entranced by', whereby the writer raises
> the reader's expectations and anticipates his or her
> response. Added to this the writer uses pronouns to
> place herself on the same side as the reader: 'And we're
> not talking ...'; 'our eyes', making the reader feel as
> though the writer understands his or her needs and
> has similar ones. This differs slightly from the use
> of the first person plural in Item 1.1 where there is a
> clearer distinction between the reader and the writer
> with the writer belonging to the 'we' who makes the
> coffee, emphasising how the firm is there to serve the
> customer.

similarity

difference

exploration

similarity

purpose and audience

purpose and audience

purpose and audience

difference

refers to text

Check your revision

What is the question?

Compare how language is used for effect in Item 1.2 and Item 2.2. Examine some examples from both Items and explain what their effects are.

Compare the ways in which presentational devices are used to make the subject seem appealing in Item 1.2 and Item 2.2. Examine some examples and evaluate their effectiveness.

The skills you need to show

- Words and phrases for comparison of texts:
  however although in the same way as similarly differently and more less in contrast with contrastingly alternatively both neither but also this differs from
- High-level reading skills include: analyse detail; explore meaning; demonstrate understanding of intended purpose and audience; evaluate effectiveness.

Making choices

Language features could include: directives; personal pronouns; adjectives; lists; present tense.

Writing an answer

Check your answer against the sample answer on page XX. Annotate where you have:

- demonstrated skills of exploration, inference and analysis
- pointed out similarities and differences
- referred to the text to support the points you make
- shown understanding of intended purpose and/or audience.

Chapter 4: Non-fiction prose

Examining the structure of newspaper articles

Activity 1

a   Who? Thousands of sceptics; What? Stage a 'mass overdose'; Where? Outside Boots stores; When? Today; Why? To protest; How? Swallow pills. All questions are answered in the first two paragraphs.

b   In the fourth paragraph. Suggests journalist assumes readers will already know its meaning.

c   Can be read quickly; can be cut easily.

Use of fact and opinion

Activity 2

a   Make sure highlighted details can be proved to be true.

b   Make sure highlighted details cannot be proved to be true or untrue.

c   It might have persuaded the reader to agree with the minority view.

d   Any valid judgement as long as it is supported.

Fact and opinion in argument

Activity 4

a   Here are just some from the first few paragraphs: 'It was the Victorians who were really obsessed with travel'; 'They lived at a time when travel really did harden the body and improve the spirit'; 'It took a rare breed of man to trudge through some malaria-infested swamp in a pith helmet'; 'Since then, travellers have thought of themselves as faintly noble'; 'they look down on mere tourists who stay in comfortable hotels and ride in air-conditioned buses'; 'To travellers it is a mark of pride to suffer as much as possible'; 'They get a perverse joy from spending all day squatting over a sordid cesspit'.

b   To make his argument appear stronger, to influence and persuade his readers.

Examining other techniques

Activity 5

a   'It took a rare breed of man to trudge through some malaria-infested swamp in a pith helmet, after the native bearers had drunk all the whisky, stolen the bully beef, and run off with the compass.' To entertain the reader and emphasize the extreme conditions faced by Victorian travellers.

b   'after the native bearers had drunk all the whisky, stolen the bully beef, and run off with the compass'

'As a rule, the only people who travel for more than a year are simpletons, social inadequates or New Zealanders.'

Explanation should be linked to the impact on the reader.

c   Any valid choice supported by relevant explanation.

Reading in the exam

Practice 1

Check your annotations against those used on the first four paragraphs.

Bias

Practice 2

Check you have annotated your answer where you have:

- examined the text closely
- explored and inferred meaning
- analysed language use.

Check your revision

Structure

- While ecotourism can be hugely beneficial, it also carries dangers.
- By the end of the third paragraph.

Fact and opinion

1 Examples of facts used to develop the argument include: 'a five-fold decline in the density of native carnivores in the areas where ecotourism was allowed'; 'Fifty thousand people now visit Antarctica every year – five times as many as in the early 1990s'; 'Nearly 180,000 people go to the Galápagos Islands'.

   Examples of opinions used to develop the argument include: 'Ecotourism can be hugely beneficial'; 'One of its most shocking findings'; 'what was once a quiet backwater became a media circus'.

   Examples of opinions being stated as fact to develop the argument include: 'One problem is sheer numbers'; 'Ecotourism can be hugely beneficial'.

2 He wishes to persuade his audience of the potential dangers, not benefits, of ecotourism.

3 'shocking'; he wants his readers to be shocked by this figure so that they will be persuaded by his argument.

Examining other techniques

1 You could have developed comments on 'a string of', 'risk', 'loved to death', 'well-meaning'. Your comments need to investigate what is implied by these terms and the intended effect on the reader.

2 Your comments could have included reference to:
   - Pantanal, Amazon, Antarctica and Galápagos all having been referred to earlier in the article, giving it a more cohesive structure;
   - the second question reinforcing the first in content and in the use of 'should' at the opening; use of emotive language, e.g. 'strike at the heart of', 'dilemma' to make the reader appreciate the seriousness of the situation;
   - the final question summarising the argument concisely for the reader; repetition of 'wildlife' stresses this as the central issue.

Bias and tone

1 Look closely at the reasons you have given for your choice. Do they refer to the text? Could you defend them?
2 Check that the evidence you have given supports your choice.

Chapter 5: More about comparison

Making a good choice

Practice 1

- Check your notes are relevant to the ways language is used for effect in Item 3 and Item 1.
- Check your notes are relevant to the ways language is used for effect in Item 3 and Item 2.
- Either choice is fine. Check that your reasons target the question.

Starting your answer

Activity 1

The second paragraph covers all of the bullet points and would make an effective opening.

Thinking about the mark scheme

Practice 2

Make sure you have covered both of the bulleted prompts in each of your rewritten paragraphs.

Structuring your answer

Practice 3

Annotate your answer to show where you have met the requirements of each bulleted point.

Check your revision

Making a good choice

Either Item 1 or 2 could be used to answer this question. Make sure the reasons for your choice are linked with the question and the high-level skills you are required to demonstrate.

Starting your answer

Annotate your answer to show where you have met the requirements of each bulleted point.

Thinking about the mark scheme

Annotate your answer to show where you have met the requirements of each bulleted point.

Chapter 8: Answering the question
Planning

Practice 1

Subject: the school day should be shortened; Purpose: to argue; Audience: the Chair of Governors; Form: a letter.

Subject: effective ways of dealing with teenage children; Purpose: to advise; Audience: parents; Form: the text for a leaflet.

Subject: reasons to support the charity of your choice; Purpose: to persuade; Audience: students at your school or college; Form: the text for a speech.

Check your revision

- 25 minutes.
- Answer the question.
- 4–5 minutes.
- Analyse the question, gather ideas, order ideas, remember range of required skills, think of interesting opening.
- Think about how to end the writing effectively.

Chapter 9: Engaging your reader
How to keep your readers' interest

Activity 2

a 8.

b 14.

c 3.

Check your revision

- Standard English.
- Rhetorical question, short sentences, description.
- Not showing the examiner sufficient variety of skills.
- Humour, anecdote, rhetorical devices, emotive use of language.

Chapter 10: Sentence structures and vocabulary

Sentence structure and vocabulary

Activity 1

First version	Improved version
To win this	Winning this
like	comparable with
gain respect	gain respect and admiration
and to gain respect	and that
an alpha male	the alpha male
Along with all the respect	Alongside respect
to choose from	from which to choose
The other think that	But there is one further desirable outcome
I would have been seen	I would be watched
not just nationwide but worldwide	across the globe
That with all the other things	So, with respect, wealth and fame
my total dream	my dream in its entirety

Check your revision

- A subject and a verb.
- A main clause makes complete sense on its own – a subordinate clause does not.
- A sentence with two or more main clauses which are joined by a conjunction such as 'and', 'so', 'or', 'but', 'because'.
- A sentence with one or more main clauses and one or more subordinate clauses.
- All kinds, as and when appropriate.
- Words and phrases well chosen for effect.
- A word used to describe the writer's attitude towards the subject and the reader; by use of inverted commas, through vocabulary choice, through imagery, through repetition.

Chapter 11: Technical accuracy

Punctuation basics

Practice 1

- Kirsty and Adam were the most unlikely couple. They had met in Cranehill Secondary School and somehow managed to stay together when all their friends had gone in different directions. They had always known their lives would be spent with each other.
- This relatively easy walk on the crags above Derwentwater in the Lake District is quite spectacular. Early September is the best time for the heather, though the great wood, currently owned by the National Trust, is worth a visit at any time of year.
- 'Stop!' shouted the guard. 'If you go any further, we will shoot you.'
- It was his first day at school and he needed to think carefully about what he should take: the shiny lizard pencil case, his best batman cape, an apple and his brand-new laser fighter.
- The warning was clear: stop or be killed.
- 'Havent you got any more money?' he asked in a whisper.
- 'No. That's all there is. We've spent everything else. We'll just have to make do.'

Punctuation: advanced

Commas

Practice 2

> *Years later, in my early twenties, I started going to a creative writing class and, after a series of assorted exercises, we were set a task. Simply to write a longer piece. A five- or six-page piece about anything at all. What could I write about? I had no idea, and then as soon as I sat down, alone in a quiet room, my stories all came back to me. Of course I'd write about the camel festival and cumin, the beggar girls, the drummer women in the square, and although when I closed my eyes I could remember, almost cinematically, my life as it was then, I realised I did have a head start. I'd practised these stories before.*
>
> Esther Freud, 'How travel shaped my life', *The Traveller's Handbook*, 2008

Plurals

Practice 3

lunches, Mondays, Christmases, beaches, radii/radiuses, ladies, atlases, inches, women, blushes, comedies, cacti/cactuses, takeaways, hoaxes, stitches, ferries, bonuses, pluses, essays, gases, arches, coaches, keys, wishes, blotches, bullies, doormen, hippopotami/hippopotamuses, media/mediums, scissors

Homonyms

Practice 4

- We're going into town where we are hoping to find something new to wear to the wedding.
- The prophet said he would bring peace to the land.
- The whole of the great hall, including the ceiling, was bathed in sunshine.
- They're not allowed to go in there until their muddy boots are removed.

Check your revision

- When a writer uses a speaker's actual words, when a writer is quoting from another text.
- Won't, shan't.
- The correct use of commas within a piece of extended writing is often an indicator of a more able student.
- One semi-colon well placed is much more effective than five semi-colons randomly placed.
- A prefix is a group of letters that can be added to the beginning of a root word to change its meaning. A suffix is a letter or group of letters that can be added to the end of a root word to change its meaning.
- Sheep, crises, tomatoes, roofs, taxis, flies.

Chapter 12: How to gain the highest grades

Writing fluently

Activities 1, 2 and 3

1 We = 16; our = 6; we've = 2; us = 1.

2 'Extreme?' refers directly to the suggestion made at the end of the first paragraph. The third paragraph starts with a suggestion as to how we can take the responsibility suggested at the end of the second paragraph. The repetition of the word 'we' at the start of the fourth paragraph makes a direct link with the ending of the third paragraph. It also moves the argument forward by suggesting a way of using the power wisely.

3 'An amazing machine, whirring and turning all day long'; 'a red rust has formed over the machine, covering the shiny steel, and destroying the screws which hold it together'; 'the machine is overheating and almost at melting point. Soon it might stop altogether'; 'we are seriously damaging the engine'; 'to learn how our machine works'; 'to begin to mend the damage we have done to it'; 'we have to wipe away the rust and oil the screws'; 'let's repair our broken engine'.

Glossary

Anecdotes: short stories about particular people or events.

Bias: a tendency towards a particular belief that can exclude other opinions.

Chronological order: the order in which something happens.

Cohesive text: a piece of writing in which the parts are closely connected to each other.

Discursive markers: words or phrases used to help structure and develop the content, for example: in a similar way; nevertheless; although.

Emotive language/loaded language: words selected to affect the feelings of the reader.

Fact: something that can be proved to be true.

Hyperbole: the deliberate exaggeration of one or more points.

Intended audience: the reader for whom the text is written.

Intended purpose: the reason or reasons for which a text is produced.

Opinion: a point of view that cannot be proved to be true or untrue.

Rhetorical devices: techniques used to influence the reader such as rhetorical questions, groups of three and repetition.

Slang: words and phrases that are used in an informal context, often linked with certain regions or groups of people.

Standard English: the variety of English most used in public communication, particularly in writing.

Tone: the mood or atmosphere created through the choice of words.